Grant Writing for Teachers

If You Can Write a Lesson Plan, You Can Write a Grant

by
Linda Karges-Bone

illustrated by Tom Heggie

Cover by Tom Heggie

Copyright © 1994, Good Apple

ISBN No. 0-86653-823-2

Printing No. 987654321

Good Apple
1204 Buchanan St., Box 299
Carthage, IL 62321-0299

Paramount Publishing

Dedication

I would like to dedicate this book to my four funding sources: those who granted me confidence, inspiration, love, and encouragement. To my sixth grade English teacher, Mrs. Mary Holderman: thank you for instilling confidence in me as a writer. To my college advisor, Dr. Jill E. McGovern: thank you for inspiring me as a teacher and a woman to take risks and to be the best. To my husband of fourteen years, Gary Bone: you are my funding source of love and you never run out. And to my savior Jesus Christ, my source of encouragement and strength.

Table of Contents

GA1515

An Introduction

I wrote *Grant Writing for Teachers* for a reason. I believe that teachers are more creative and powerful than they know. Too often teachers drift into a belief that they are powerless to make significant changes in their schools and communities. They are wrong.

Teachers can move beyond the confines of the classroom and make two important contributions that will bring positive change in the lives of students. Teachers can seize the role that should have always been theirs: that of curriculum designer. And teachers can help to generate funding to propel that same curriculum. Grant writing can play an integral role in both transitions.

However, transitions can be troubling to parents, teachers, and administrators. So, let's look at the words of one who thrived on change and shared an invigorating vision for school reform, John Dewey.

In *Experience and Education* (1938) John Dewey wrote, "A genuine purpose always starts with an impulse." Grant writing is like that. A teacher has a brainstorm, a "wild hair," an impulse. He or she transforms that impulse into a proposal that brings excitement and enhancement into the classroom, the school, and the community. Grant writing is the business of teachers because teachers are the ones with the impulse and imagination to make change happen. In 1938 John Dewey said something that is fresh even today: "Conservatives as well as radicals in education are profoundly discontented with the present educational system taken as a whole." If you are not content with your teaching situation, then make a change. Go with your impulse. Follow your dreams. Write a grant.

Linda Karges-Bone

GA1515

Foreword

Educators of today are searching for innovative programs that enhance student learning and achievement. Teachers and administrators are willing to take risks and implement new ideas to improve instruction. Today's economy makes it increasingly hard to provide the resources and materials necessary to implement new programs. School administrators and teachers are challenged to be creative in their search for available funding sources. One of the best avenues for funding is through grant writing.

As a principal of a successful elementary school, one that has received state and national recognition, I have found grant writing to be one of the major keys of our school's success. The school has been the recipient of two NDN grants that have significantly impacted our instructional program and spearheaded us into many new directions.

The easy steps and techniques Linda Karges-Bone offers in this book enable the first-time grant writer to develop and produce a successful proposal with ease. She cuts through the technical jargon that usually intimidates teachers. Everything is outlined in easy-to-follow steps and procedures.

Motivating teachers to write grants is not an easy task. Recently, our school contracted a day with Linda Karges-Bone to work with teachers and help them simplify the grant-writing process. Her enthusiasm and expertise motivated and provided teachers with the confidence and knowledge to create a successful proposal. Linda Karges-Bone's simple techniques for grant writing eliminated obstacles that have discouraged us on many occasions.

I am excited that Linda decided to share her successful grant-writing tips in this book with others so that quality educational programs can continue to be funded. Grant writing not only stimulates teachers to look at current research data, but it helps to evaluate our current educational programs. Even if a grant is not funded, change usually occurs in the classroom.

Opportunities for the grant proposal experience outlined in this book help develop a network for teachers sharing ideas that continues beyond the grant-writing process. I strongly encourage educators to participate in the grant-writing process. It not only serves as a vehicle for change in the school but is a great way to foster teamwork and provide an avenue for funding quality instructional programs.

Patsy Pye

GA1515

1

If you can write a lesson plan, you can write a grant. "No way!" You are thinking, "I can't possibly tackle something as complex and technical as a grant proposal. You need special training for that kind of writing. Schools hire experts to write grants. Teachers aren't grant writers." Wrong! Teachers can write grants. Remember your logic from college? A + B = C. Here's the formula.

Teachers write lesson plans every day.
Grants, in their simplest form, are like lesson plans.
So, teachers can write grants.

Grant Writing for Teachers will take you through the steps required to write a fundable grant proposal. Working page by page, you can create a fundable, creative proposal that will make a difference.

GA1515

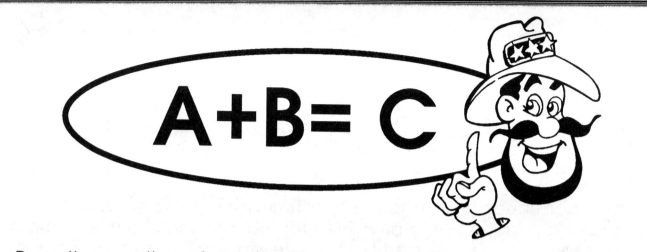

Does the mention of grant writing send you into a nervous tailspin? Just calm down and think about the fact that grant writing draws heavily upon skills that you already have and on one skill especially . . . writing lesson plans. Let's look at grant writing from the perspective of skills that you as a teacher already possess and use every day. This is part A of the A + B = C formula.

Skills of Teachers   **Check Yourself**

 1. Planning   _____
 2. Organizing   _____
 3. Communicating   _____
 4. Creating   _____
 5. Making Learning Interesting   _____
 6. Testing New Ideas   _____
 7. Evaluating Progress   _____
 8. Finding New Ways to Pay for Things   _____
 9. Being a Self-Starter   _____
10. Utilizing Community Resources   _____

Now, write a brief response to this statement: "I can become a grant writer because I already have qualities and skills such as . . ."

_____

_____

_____

_____

GA1515

A + B = C

Let's continue the process of understanding grant writing as it applies to teachers or to any writer for that matter. Grant writing is a process, not just a product. You are engaging in a process of *designing a plan for teaching* that will require money. If A + B = C, then this is the **B** part. A grant is like a lesson plan. In what ways is a grant like a lesson plan? Mark each item with an *x* or a + mark.

Compare and Contrast

	Lesson Plan	Grant
Has objectives		
Lists materials		
Outlines steps or procedures		
Requires assessment or evaluation		
Is based on learning needs of students		
Draws on teacher creativity		

Answer: You should have a + by each item. Go on to the next page. You are ready for part C.

4

GA1515

A + B = C

Here we are, at part C of the A + B = C formula for becoming a teacher who also writes grants. The C stands for **can**. You **can** write a successful grant. Pick up a pencil and fill in the blanks (using your own words) to explain (or in "Grantese," justify) your formula for success as a grant writer.

The "I Can" Formula for Grant Writing

Once upon a time, there was a _____ grade teacher

named _____, who had been in the profession for

_____ years. He/She was frustrated because each year

the money crunch at school seemed to become _____.

"I have a dozen _____ ideas," said the teacher, "but

no dollars to put them into action. I would write a grant to pay for

them, but it is too _____! I would need to write objectives

and goals; that's not too _____. And there would be

a section on justifying need. Well, I could fill a book on that one. My

students are weak in _____, _____, and

_____. And then there's evaluation. I use _____

and _____ as evaluation tools all the time. Is that all? Maybe

I *will* go ahead and write that grant. And the teacher did and got

funded for $ _____ and lived happily ever after at

_____ school.

GA1515

Brainstorm

Although your final *product* will be clear and concise, the actual *process* of "granting" is often a brainstorm. In brainstorming, you generate as many ideas as possible, rejecting none and considering all. At this point, ask yourself "Will I work alone or with a group?" Many successful grants have been written by a team. For your first brainstorm, gather a group (two to five total) of teachers and even an administrator who would like to work on a proposal. Use these lines to brainstorm lots of ideas.

1. Who wants to work on the grant?

_____

_____

_____

_____

(Note: Think about including special area teachers such as music, art, band, media, and special education.)

2. When can we set aside time to work on our grant together and individually?

_____

_____

_____

_____

(Note: Several successful "grant schools" regularly hire substitutes in order to release a team of teachers to write grants.)

GA1515

More Brainstorm

3. Did we include business partners, parent volunteers, or district office personnel who may have experience in the area that our grant will focus on?

_____

_____

_____

_____

(Note: A "Letter of Support" is valuable. See Chapter 5.)

4. What tools and materials will we need to write a grant? Who in our team will find these resources?

_____

_____

_____

_____

(Note: A complete list is offered in this section of the book.)

5. What do we want a grant for? Be creative, not specific at this point.

_____

_____

_____

GA1515

Materials Checklist ✔✔

Check off the items on this list that you have, can borrow, or can find. Gather these materials after your brainstorming session.

Item	Yes/No	Source/Who Will Find
Legal pads		
Pencils		
Dictionary/thesaurus		
Word processor		
Printer		
Professional journals and teaching magazines		
Catalogs of teaching supplies		
Test scores for our grade and entire school		
Newspaper articles about our topic or area of interest		
Portfolios of student work in the area of weakness		
Coffee, soda, snacks		

GA1515

Principals Can Promote Grants

Principals can create an atmosphere of excitement about grant writing that encourages teachers to take the plunge and bring in important funding for schools. The following suggestions have been successfully applied by principals that I have personally consulted with, and together we have generated over $1,000,000 in grants for schools. How many ideas can you adopt in your school? Remember, the investment in time and resources is usually returned with interest and more!

The Principal's Corner

1. Provide release time by using substitutes or parent volunteers or administrators to cover classes while teachers work on a grant proposal.

2. Pay teachers an honorarium to submit a proposal. The PTA might raise funds for these honoraria.

3. Provide child care and snacks for children while teachers work after school on a proposal.

4. Bring in a consultant to help teachers focus their ideas for a proposal.

5. Set up a "Grant Center" with the items listed on the previous page, and keep it stocked with bulletins and ideas for grants.

6. Provide secretarial help to proofread and type the final drafts of proposals for teachers.

7. Reward teachers who write grants with praise and professional letters that can be used for promotion.

8. Learn to write grants yourself and really provide a model for teachers to follow.

9. Collaborate with a local teacher education college to submit a grant jointly or to provide graduate credit for a grant writing course.

10. Adjust schedules so that teachers can use their planning periods more effectively to write grants.

11. Use in-service days to provide time and support for teachers who are writing grants.

12. Give copies of *Grant Writing for Teachers* to your faculty during Teacher Appreciation Week.

****

Now, sketch out *your* plan for generating grants and motivating teachers to write grants.

_____

_____

_____

_____

_____

_____

_____

GA1515

Attitude Check ✔

At this point, you may be thinking "Okay, I could learn to write a grant, but why would a teacher want to write a grant? Money is the only incentive, right?"

Wrong! Take a look at these important reasons for writing a grant, and rate your response to each one.

Grant Writers' Attitude Inventory

Grant writing builds professional status.	Seldom	Sometimes	Often
Grant writing encourages creativity.	Seldom	Sometimes	Often
Grant writing could lead to a promotion or raise.	Seldom	Sometimes	Often
Grant writing helps to focus my teaching style and philosophy.	Seldom	Sometimes	Often
Grant writing could help me move up the career ladder.	Seldom	Sometimes	Often
Grant writing might help me in graduate schoolwork.	Seldom	Sometimes	Often
Grant writing leads me to read more professional articles.	Seldom	Sometimes	Often
Grant writing encourages cooperation within a faculty.	Seldom	Sometimes	Often

GA1515

Chapter Review

As you complete the first chapter of *Grant Writing for Teachers*, you should be feeling more confident and eager about writing your own proposal. The "attitude inventory" really wraps up Chapter 1 nicely, so let's turn now to a list of why grant proposals fail to help you. Focus on the next eleven chapters. Think of these pitfalls to success as you work through the next sections.

Why Grant Proposals Fail

- The problem is not clearly identified or is not significant enough to support a grant.
- Too much jargon is used in the narrative making the proposal unclear.
- Vagueness in any section weakens the grant: insufficient data in the needs section or an unclear description of the target group.
- Sloppy objectives and poorly defined evaluation criteria will kill your proposal.
- An inappropriate time schedule or an unrealistic budget sends up a red flag to the readers.
- Overly ambitious projects that are simply too much to accomplish given your time and resources will be dismissed.
- Simply submitting your proposal to the wrong agency or foundation can be an error. Check out what is being funded first.

GA1515

GA1515

Definition of a Grant

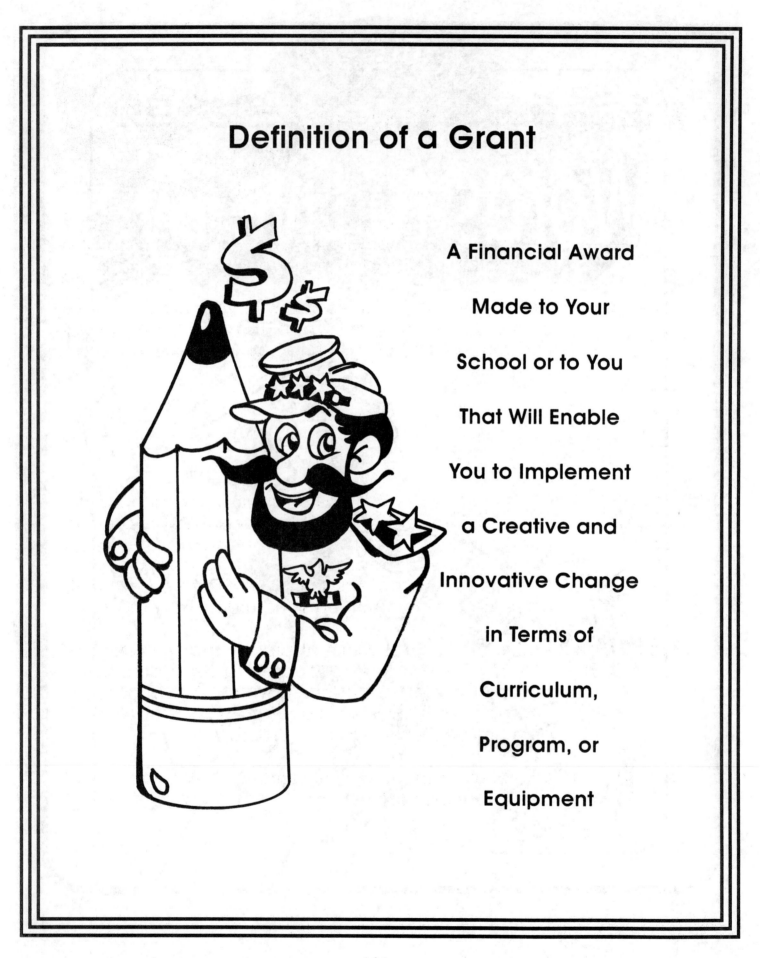

A Financial Award

Made to Your

School or to You

That Will Enable

You to Implement

a Creative and

Innovative Change

in Terms of

Curriculum,

Program, or

Equipment

GA1515

A Grant Writer's Glossary

Abstract: A brief overview of your proposal. No more than one page long and containing the bare essentials and a description of the goal and outcomes.

Addendum: Extra pages that you include with your grant, such as letters of support or test scores. These must be labeled (Addendum VII) and referenced within the narrative of the grant.

Application: The forms used by the funding agency to submit your proposal. You should write or call the funding source *before* you begin writing the grant.

Authorized Signature: This is the signature of the person who is legally responsible for your institution. In many schools both the principal and superintendent and sometimes even school board members will need to sign your proposal. Example: Dr. Louise Smith, principal, completed the authorized signature for my proposal.

Block Grants: This refers to large sums of money that the state or federal government allocates to fund a specific need. Example: The federal government will allocate 2.5 million dollars in a block grant to schools that provide after-school care for children.

Brief: This refers to the length of sentences that you should use in your proposal.

Budget: The financial plan for your grant. You should use whole dollar amounts only and provide a detailed itemized list in addition to the raw numbers.

Capitation Grant: This kind of grant is based on the number of students that you will be serving in your project. Example: The capitation grant will provide $2 per day for each child enrolled in the Head Start project.

Client Group: This is the correct term for the audience that you will be serving with your proposal. Example: Our client group is third grade boys who have already failed one grade level.

Consultant: A professional who is not part of your regular faculty, but who comes in periodically to provide specific expertise. Example: We hired a consultant to give a series of workshops on parenting skills as part of our grant.

Continuation Grant: This kind of grant is automatically funded over a period of several years as long as the grantee is meeting the program objectives. Don't count on these kinds of grants; they are few and far between.

Contract: A legal document that specifies work or services that will be provided as part of your grant. These are attached to the itemized budget. Example: We have a contract to pay the professional storyteller who will be part of our school-wide literature grant.

Coordinator: This person may be in charge of the entire project (see Project Director) or, in a large grant, he or she may be responsible for one site or one strand of the project. Example: Dr. Jones is the project director but Ms. Smith is the coordinator of the school testing site.

GA1515

Cost Sharing: This is a method of "matching money" in which you, the grantee, agree to put up a certain sum of or even "in-kind" dollars in order to make your proposal more attractive. Example: As part of our cost sharing, we agreed to pay one half of the director's salary out of our PTA funds.

Cover Letter: This is a formal letter that you attach to the front of your application/proposal when you submit it. A sample cover letter is included in this section.

Deadline: The date after which your proposal will not be accepted. Usually a postmark will not suffice; the funding group will require that it be on the desk by 4:00 p.m. that day.

Direct Cost: This is the whole dollar amount necessary to fund your project and includes cash money only, not indirect cost.

Dissemination: How will you tell other teachers about the success of your project or share your model for learning or your new curriculum? You must outline a plan for dissemination in the narrative. (See also Exportable Product.)

Effective Date: The date the award is made.

Equipment: The definition of equipment is usually an item that has a unit value of more than $500 and can be used for more than two years; otherwise, you call the item "supplies." Example: A computer is listed as equipment, but the software package is a supply.

Evaluation: This refers to both qualitative and quantitative assessment of the project. Did it work? Did you meet your goals? How will you document your evaluation?

Expendable: This refers to items that are useless after just one year, such as paper supplies.

Expiration Date: This refers to the day on which your funding cycle ends.

Exportable Product: A part of dissemination: you prepare something, such as a presentation, curriculum guide, brochure, or even a videotape, that would tell other teachers, parents, and administrators how to implement your project.

Fee: A negotiated sum of money that you pay to an individual or business for a service. Typically, a contract is required before the grant can pay such a fee.

Final Report: This is a summary of your project's outcomes in terms of the program, evaluation, budget, and personnel. Take your time and make the report thorough; it can affect future funding.

Foundation: A private group or organization that awards funds for charitable or research purposes. Example: The Coca-Cola Foundation funds research in teacher education and school reform.

Goals: The broad outcomes that you expect from your project. Goals are not measurable, but objectives must be! Example: Our goal is to promote family involvement in schools.

Grant: An award of financial or other kinds of equipment or assistance that is based on a proposal for change or research. A grant does not have to be "paid back."

Grantee: This is the agency or individual that receives the award/grant.

GA1515

Grantor:	This is the agency or foun-dation that gives the award/grant.
Grant Period:	The time between the effective date and the expiration date in which you carry out your program or research.

Guidelines:	These are the directions that you must follow in preparing an application for funding. Follow them exactly as outlined or you will lose points as the reader evaluates your proposal.
Honorarium:	A monetary amount paid to a prestigious speaker or advisor who has given you assistance in the program. This is not a fee.
Indirect Cost:	This is the overhead that your school would have to pay in order to support a grant (electricity, rent for space, parking, etc.). Typically, the school can keep an agreed-upon amount (5% to 10%) of the award in order to implement the proposal.
In-Kind:	This refers to a contribution of service or items that your school donates instead of a monetary sum, in order to help fund the project. Example: One third of our guidance counselor's time will be contributed as in-kind to the grant. (See three-line budget for more information.)
Justification:	See Need Statement.
Letter of Intent:	You send a letter of intent before you write or submit a grant to an agency or foundation. This way, you will not waste time and energy by preparing a grant that does not follow the guidelines. (See above.)

GA1515

Letter of Support: This refers to a simple letter that you attach as an addendum to your proposal. The letter would be from an "expert" or supporter of your project who tells why he or she believes that your program should be funded. Example: Dr. Laura Jones wrote a letter of support for my whole language proposal. She is a professor at the local university and specializes in children's literature.

Matching Funds: This refers to a dollar amount that the grantee or other outside party contributes toward the project.

Narrative: This is the written portion of your grant. It is the story of who, what, when, where, how, and why. Every grant has two parts: a narrative and a budget. Often, the grant guidelines will specify that your narrative cannot be more than ten pages. They aren't kidding.

Need Statement: The part of the grant in which you explain, using both qualitative and quantitative data, why you should be funded. Remember to outline your problems and give data to verify or justify the problem areas. Sometimes called "justification."

Objectives: Just as in lesson plans, these are specific, measurable aims for your projects. Keep in mind that every objective must have a matching outcome to measure it.

Outcome: This refers to the expected results of your project. Example: We expect that reading test scores as measured by the Metropolitan Reading Test will increase by ten points for each student. Outcomes must match objectives.

Outside Evaluator: This is an unbiased, professional consultant who is brought in to do the evaluation of your project. Typically, an outside evaluator is advisable in large grants ($100,000) and assures the grantor of quality and integrity in your evaluation.

GA1515

Program Officer:	This individual is legally responsible for the financial and funding parts of the grant.
Project:	This term refers to the activities that you will carry out as part of the grant.
Project Director:	This individual is responsible for the activities involved in the grant, including the evaluation and follow-up. May also be called a coordinator.
Prospectus:	A draft of your proposal that may sometimes be called a preliminary proposal.
Qualitative Data:	The results of attitude inventories, case studies, and question-naires tell you how people are feeling or behaving. These can be used for needs assessment or evaluation.
Quantitative Data:	Statistics. Number crunching. Use test scores or demo-graphics to justify the need for or outcomes of your grant. It is a good idea to mix both qualitative and quantitative data to paint a thorough picture of your situation.
Reader:	A consultant or staff member who reads and evaluates the quality of proposals. Typically, points are given for each section of the grant and then a committee votes on those proposals that have made it past the cutoff point.
RFP:	This is a kind of memo that agencies or foundations send out to solicit proposals. It stands for *request for proposals*. You should send a letter of intent (see above) and request an application packet.

GA1515

Seed Money: A small award that is given to help you get a project started or to study the need for a full project. Example: We were given $5000 seed money to study the need for an alternative assessment program in our school.

Site Visit: One or more evaluators from the foundation or agency visit your school to either review the facilities for the purpose of funding you in the first place, or as part of the evaluation after you have been funded. Be very nice to them and make a good impression. It matters more than you know.

Summary: The portion of the narrative in which you describe who, what, when, where, how, and why, but do it briefly. Let the reader know what this proposal is about. Sharpen the reader's appetite.

Terms and Conditions: The legal requirements that you must agree to before accepting the grant award.

Three-Column Budget: A kind of budget in which you show three sources for funding: the grantor (agency or foundation), outside funding (matching funds from a business partner or supporter), and your own in-kind support.

Glossary Review Puzzle

Did you find the glossary to be a challenge? Let's take a few minutes to review the terms by completing this crossword puzzle. Don't peek!

Across

1. Philanthropic group
4. Data such as questionnaires and case studies
6. Gives the problem area and convinces the reader to fund you
7. Financial plan for the grant
10. Evaluators come to review your progress
12. Broadly, what do you expect from the project?
13. A first draft
14. One who awards the grant
15. Must be attached to the grant with Roman numerals marking the pages
16. One who receives the grant

Down

1. You turn this in when the project is complete to tell what happened
2. Whole dollar amount of the project
3. Services donated by your institution in lieu of dollars
4. Data such as statistics
5. The written part of the grant
8. A one-page summary of the grant
9. A small grant to get you started on a major project
11. Expected results: specific

Choose the Right Word

Grant writing is part science and part art. You learn the method of linking important pieces and including specific ingredients–that is the science. But choosing the right words to describe your project–that is art. Choosing and using the right words help you to set the tone of your narrative. Aim for a lively yet professional tone and a clear, concise style of writing. By using short yet animated words, you can achieve this goal. While writing the narrative, keep a dictionary and thesaurus handy, and consult this word list for appropriate choices.

A Words

abandon
abundant
accelerate
acceptable
accessible
accommodate
accurate
acquire
active
adapt
adventure
advertise
advocate (verb)
advocate (noun)
affect
afford to
after all (transition words)
aggressive
agree
aim
allocate
alter
altogether (transition words)
ambitious
ammunition
amplify
analyze
animate
answer
apply
appreciation for
approval/approve

arrive at
artistic
ask
assemble
assess
assessment
assimilate
associate
assume
attack
attempt
attuned to
authentic
aware

B Words

backlash
backslide
basic
basis
bear out
becoming
beget
begin
behalf
behavior
belief/believe
beneficial
benefit
better
blame
blast
blemish

Choose the Right Word

blessing
block
blunder
bold
booming
bored
boundless
bountiful
bracing
brainy
branch out
bridge (verb)
brighten
bring
browse
buckle down
bulldoze
business
busy

C Words

cage
calculate
call
camaraderie
campaign
cancel
candid
canvas (as a verb)
cap (as a verb)
capacity
capitalize on
captivating
capture
care
careful
carry
carry out
cast off
catalyst
catch
catchy
categorical
categorize
causal

caution
cautious
celebrate
certainly (transition word)
champion
chance
change
channel
characteristic
charge
charter
chase
chasm
cheapen
check
chiefly
choice
choose
chronic
chronological
circular
citation
claim
clarity
clash
class
classic
clear-cut
clearly (transition word)
clever
cliché
closure
cogent
cohesive
cohort
collaborate
collapse
collect
combat
combine
command
commend
comment on
commit
comparative

Choose the Right Word

compassion
compel
complacent
complete
complex
complicate
component
compress (as a verb)
compromise
compulsory
concentrate
concise
concur
conducive to
confident
confirm
conform
confuse
congruent
consequence
consequently (transition word)
constant
continue
controversy
convert
convey
convince
cooperate
coordinate
correct
create
creative
credible
crucial
cultivate
curious
cut (verb)

D Words

dangerous
dare
daring
dash
dated (old)
dazzle

deal
debate
decent
decide
decision
decisive
declare
decline
decrease
deduct
deep-rooted
defend
defiant
deficient
definite
delegate
deliberate
deliver
demanding
demonstrate
departure
dependable
deplorable
deposit
design
desirable
detail (noun and verb)
detect
determined
detriment
development
dialogue
differ
differences
diffuse
dignity
diligence
direct
direction
disadvantaged
discern
discipline
discordant
discovery
discrepancy

GA1515

Choose the Right Word

discriminate
disjointed
disparity
display
dissatisfaction
dissension
distinct
distribute
divergent
diversify
doubtful
draft (verb)
drain
dramatic
draw (verb)
drive
dubious
duplicate
dwindle
dynamic

E Words
eager
early on
earmark
earn
easily
eclectic
educate
effect
effective
efficient
effort
elaborate
elevate
eliminate
elusive
embrace (verb)
empower
encompass
encounter (verb)
encouragement
endeavor
endure
engage (verb)

enhance
enlighten
enormous
enterprise
enthusiastic
equality
equitable
equity
essential
evaluate
evaluation
event
evidence
exact
examine
example
exceed
excellent
exceptional
exchange
execute
exemplary
exercise (verb)
exhaust (verb)
exhibit (verb)
expect
expectation
experiment
expert
explain
explicit
expose
express
extend
extensive
extraordinary
extreme
exuberance

F Words
facilitate
factor
faddish
fail
fair

GA1515

Choose the Right Word

fairly
fallacy
familiar
family
feasible
feeling
fertile
fight
fill
finance
find
finite
firm
fitting (adjective)
fix
flagrant
fledging
flexible
flood (verb)
flourish
fluctuate
foggy
follow
foolish
force
forceful
forerunner
fortify
forward
fragmentary
frame (verb)
frenzy
frequent
fresh
fruition
frustration
full
full-fledged
full-scale
fun
functional
fund
fundamental
furor
fusion

futile
future

G Words
gain
galvanize
gap
gauge (verb)
generally (transition word)
generate
generous
genius
genuine
germane
gimmick
give
glaring
govern
gradual
grandstand
grant
grave (adjective)
guarantee
guide (verb)
gutsy

H Words
halt
handy
haphazard
happen
happy
harbor (verb)
hard-nosed
harmonious
harsh
hazard
healthy
heartfelt
heighten
help
heroic
hesitant
highly
hold

GA1515

Choose the Right Word

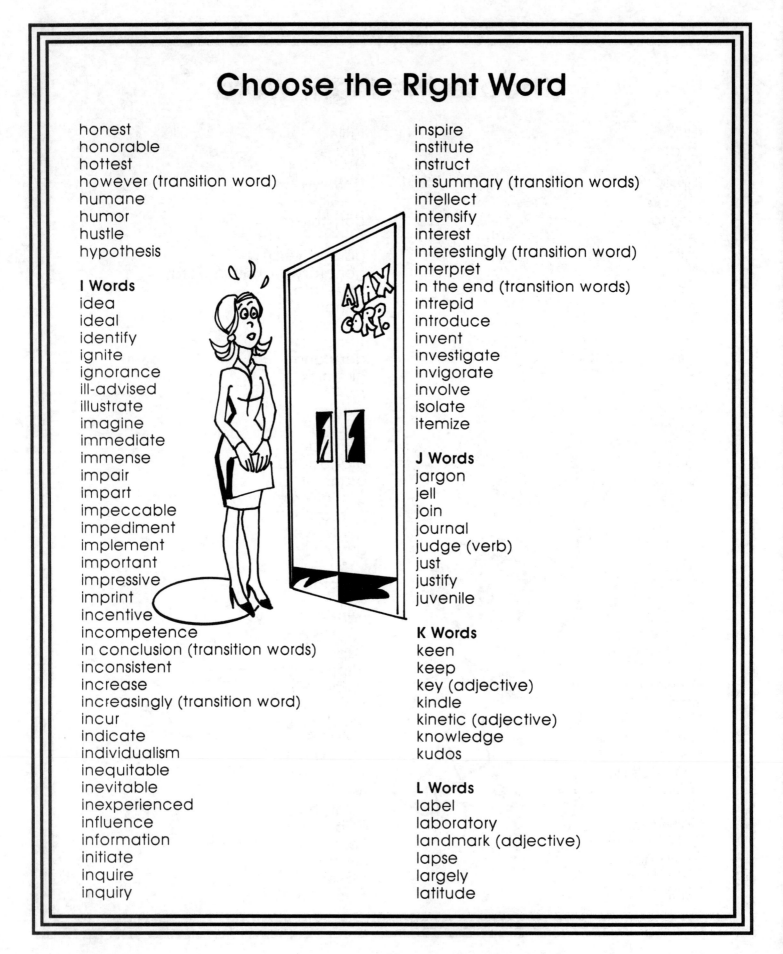

honest
honorable
hottest
however (transition word)
humane
humor
hustle
hypothesis

I Words
idea
ideal
identify
ignite
ignorance
ill-advised
illustrate
imagine
immediate
immense
impair
impart
impeccable
impediment
implement
important
impressive
imprint
incentive
incompetence
in conclusion (transition words)
inconsistent
increase
increasingly (transition word)
incur
indicate
individualism
inequitable
inevitable
inexperienced
influence
information
initiate
inquire
inquiry

inspire
institute
instruct
in summary (transition words)
intellect
intensify
interest
interestingly (transition word)
interpret
in the end (transition words)
intrepid
introduce
invent
investigate
invigorate
involve
isolate
itemize

J Words
jargon
jell
join
journal
judge (verb)
just
justify
juvenile

K Words
keen
keep
key (adjective)
kindle
kinetic (adjective)
knowledge
kudos

L Words
label
laboratory
landmark (adjective)
lapse
largely
latitude

GA1515

Choose the Right Word

laudable
law
lax
lead (verb)
leadership
lecture
legacy
legitimatize
lessen
lethargy
liberal
liberate
lift
limitless
link (verb)
literally
lobby (verb)
long-range
look
lucid
luxury

M Words
magic
magnetic
magnify
mainly (transition word)
mainstay
maintain
make
manage
mandate
maneuver
manifest
mark (verb)
mask (verb)
master (verb)
matchless
mature
maximum
meager
mean (average)
measure
mechanism
mediate

meet
member
mend
mental
merge
mesh
method
methodical
mild
minimum
mix
model (verb and noun)
moderate
modus operandi
monitor
moreover (transition word)
muddle
multiple
multiply
mutual

N Words
name
narrate
native
neat
necessity
need
needy
negate
negative
negotiate
net (verb)
network (verb)
neutral
nominal
noncommittal
nonsense
norm
notable
notice
now (transition word)
nudge
nullify
number (verb)

31

Choose the Right Word

nurture

O Words
object (verb)
objective
obscure
observe
obsolete
obstacle
obvious
obviously (transition word)
odyssey
official
offspring
open-minded
operate
opportune
opportunity
opposition
optimistic
optimum
order
ordinary
organize
original
orthodox
otherwise (transition word)
outcome
outline (verb)
overall (transition word)
overlap
overwhelming
ownership

P Words
package (verb)
painstaking
pair (verb)
paltry
pandemonium
paradigm
paradigm shift
paradox
paradoxically (transition word)
parallel (verb)

par for the course
parity
partial
participant
particularly (transition word)
pass
passionate
patient
pattern
peak (verb)
pedagogic
pedagogy
peerless
penetrate
perception
perennial
performance
peripheral
perpetuate
persist
personality
perspective
persuasion
pertinent
phase out
philosophy
plainly (transition word)
play
plea
plentiful
plunge
point out
point to
polarize
polish (verb or noun)
ponder
pool (verb)
popular
position
positive
positively (transition word)
potent
potential
poverty

Choose the Right Word

power
practice
pragmatic
praise
precedence
precise
preferable
prerequisite
pressure
prestigious
presumption
prevail
priceless
primarily (transition word)
primary
prime
priority
produce
profess
progressive (adjective)
project (noun or verb)
promote
proof
proponent
propose (verb)
protect
protract
provide
prudence
public
pull
purchase
purposeful
puzzle (verb)

Q Words
qualify
quality
quasi
quest
question
quick
quota
quotation
quote

R Words
race
raise
ramification
rampant
rank (verb)
rapid
rare
rarely (transition word)
reach
react
readiness
realistically (transition word)
reality
realm
reason
reasonable
rebound
recall
receive
receptive
reciprocal (adjective)
recognize
recommend
record (verb)
recovery
rectify
reduce
refer
refine
reflect
reflective (adjective)
reflex
reform
refreshing
regarding (transition word)
regenerate
register
regress
regulate
reinforce
relate to
relatively speaking (transition words)
relieve
remarkable

GA1515

Choose the Right Word

remedial
render
renovate
repair
repeat
report
represent
require
rescue
research
resilient
resist
resolve
resourceful
respectable
responsive
restore
restriction
revamp
reveal
reverse
revolutionary
reward
rewarding
rhetorical
right
rightly (transition word)
rigor
robust

S Words
sample (verb)
satisfactory
savor
scale (verb)
scant
scarcity
scholarship
scientific
score
screen (verb)
scrutinize
search
seek
seize

select
sensible
sensitive
separate
sequence
serious
setting
sham
sharpen
shock
shortly (transition word)
sidetrack
significant
simple
simulate
sincere
society
solid
special
specify
speculate
sponsor
spread (verb)
spur (verb)
squelch
standards
stimulate
stipulation
strategic
strengthen
strike
struggle
study
subject
subtle
successful
suggest
summarize
superior
supplementary
supportive
surely (transition word)
survey
sustain
synthesis

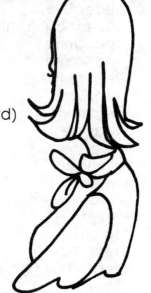

34

GA1515

Choose the Right Word

systemize

T Words
take
talk
tap
teacher
teaching
team player
teamwork
temporary
tendency
tenure
term
terminate
territory
theory
therapeutic
therefore (transition word)
think
thorough
thoughtful
threatening
tighten
together
tolerate
track (verb)
traditionally (transition word)
transfer
translate
treasure
tremendous
trend
trim
trivial
true
trust
try
turn
typically (transition word)

U Words
ultimate
unavoidable
unbridled

uncertain
uncommon
unconditional
unconventional
undeniable
undercurrent
understand
understanding
undertake
undo
uneven
unique
unit
unite
unprecedented
unsatisfactory
uplift
uproar
urge
use
useful
utilize

V Words
valid
validate
valuable
values
vantage
variable
variation
varying
vent (verb)
venture
veracity
verify
vibrant
view (verb)
viewpoint
vigilant
vigorous
violate
virtually
vision
vital

GA1515

Choose the Right Word

vitality
vivid
vocal
volatile
vulnerable

zero hour
zest
zone
zoom

W Words
wager
waken
wake up
wanting
ward off
warn
warrant
waste
watchdog
watertight
way
weaken
weave
wedge
weighty
welcome
well-balanced
wellness
wholeness
wholly
widen
widespread
wisdom
withstand
work
workable
work of art
write
wrong

Y-Z Words
yardstick
yearly
yield
youth
zap
zeal
zealous

GA1515

Chapter Review

Let's review your progress through the first two chapters of *Grant Writing for Teachers*.

In Chapter 1, you mentally primed yourself to tackle a grant. What key words do you recall from that experience? _____ and _____ and _____ are important.

In Chapter 2, you were introduced to a glossary of grant writing terms and to a list of words that can improve your writing style. Now, jot down a few terms from the glossary that were completely new to you: _____ and _____ and _____ and _____ were new to me.

Now, you are ready to proceed to Chapter 3, which deals with setting the focus of your grant. Get ready to dream a little bit and have fun as you set off on a grant writing odyssey. (Did you recall that last word from the list?)

GA1515

Step One: The Topic

Grant writing is competitive. Dollars are scarce and are awarded to the surefooted and carefully crafted proposals. How can you make your proposal clean and clear? The first step is to pinpoint your topic. Be sure of what it is you are writing for and about! You have to be specific. It is wise to be timely in your choice of topic. Try this process.

On the lines below, list five words that describe the focus of your proposal. Limit yourself to one word per line.

Example: The focus of my grant is:

1. _____

2. _____

3. _____

4. _____

5. _____

Now, turn the page and scan the list of "200 Hot Topics for Grants." Did you find any of your topics on the list? Perhaps your topic might fit into one of these areas. If your topic is applicable to one of the "200," then go to pages 55-57, "Writing a Project Summary." If your topic is not on the "200" list, turn to page 43, "Fine-Tuning Your Topic and Target."

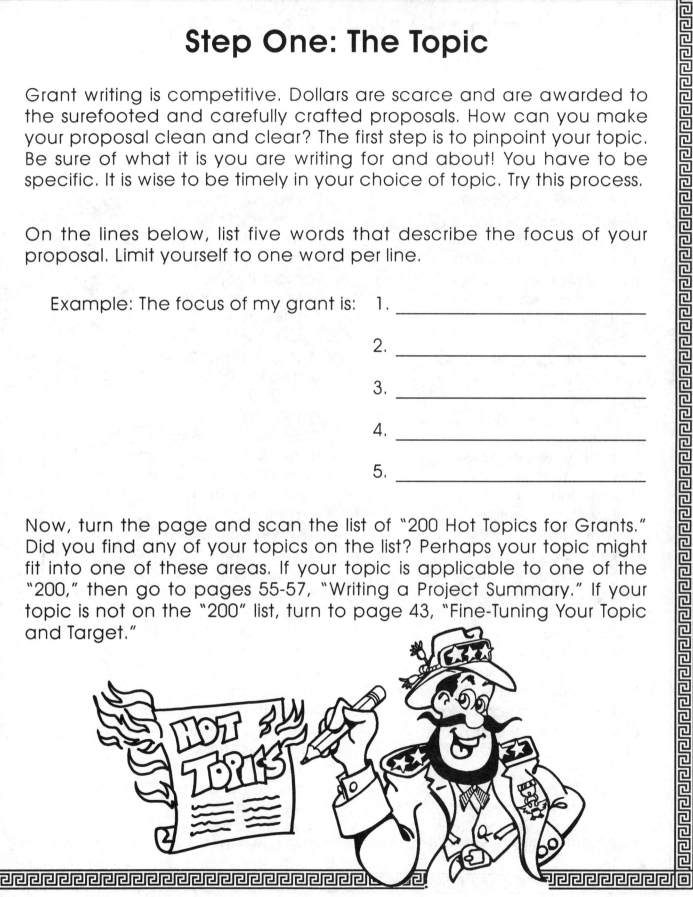

GA1515

200 Hot Topics for Grants

Activities Integrating Math and Science
AIDS Education
Alphabet Units
Alternative Assessment
Anthropology
Apartheid
Architecture
Art Applied to Basic Skills
At-Risk Children
Attention Deficit Disorder
Authors in the Classroom
Baltic Republics
Bears (as a theme)
Behavior Management
Big Books
Black History
Block Play
The Body
Book Making
The Brain
Breathing (healthy lungs)
Broken Families
Career Planning
Children's Literature
Cinema in the Classroom
Citizenship Programs
Computers in the Classroom
Cooking for Basic Skills
Critical Thinking Skills
Cultural Diversity
Cultural Literacy
Currency and Banking
Dance and Movement Programs
Developmentally Appropriate Education
Dinosaurs (as a theme)
Disabled and Delayed Children
Discipline
Divorce Support Groups
Drug Intervention Projects
Early Childhood (anything)
Early Intervention (any kind)

Ecology
Economics for Kids
Ecosystems
Elections
Electronics/Electricity
Environmental Policy
Erasmus and Others
Ethnic Studies
Fables and Folklore
Family Values
Famine
Famous People
Foreign Languages
Fossil Finds
Fossil Fuels
Games for the Classroom
Gems and Rocks
Geography
Geometry
Glaciers (the Arctic)
Habitats (human, animal)
Hands-On (anything)
Hearing Impaired
Hispanic Culture
History (nonwestern)
Holidays Around the World
Homeless Children
Hurricanes (storms)
Hurried Children
Iambic Pentameter (poetry)
Immunization Projects
Industry
Information Skills
Integrated Curricula
Inventors, Inventions
Japanese Studies
Journalism
Judges (the law)
Juvenile Literature
Juvenile Violence
Kilometers (metrics)

200 Hot Topics for Grants

Kindergarten
Koalas (Australia)
Kuwait
Laboratories in the Classroom
Language Development
Latin American Studies
Latin (as a language)
Learning Disabled Kids
Leaves (botany)
Legends and Myths
Longitude and Latitude (maps)
Magna Carta (and others)
Magnets
Mammals
Mathematics (applied)
Meteorology
Middle School Programs
Motivation Projects
Music and Basic Skills
Native American Studies
Natural Resources
Nature Lore
Newspapers in Education
Nickels and Pennies (money)
Nobel Prize Winners
Nuclear Issues
Number Systems
Nutrition
Obese Children
Oceanography
Orient
Original Writing and Creativity
Ornithology
Orthology (spelling)
Othello and Other Plays
Overcoming Stress
Oxygen and Other Gases (science)
Ozone Layer
Paragraphs (writing skills)
Parenting Programs

Pen Pals (foreign and local)
Persian Gulf
Personal Body Safety
Photography
Photosynthesis (gardening projects)
Portfolios
Power and Energy
Presidents (wives)
Pride in Oneself
Pride in One's School
Problem Solving
Publishing
Quakes (earth)
Quasars and Other Phenomena
Quotes from Famous Speeches and Texts
Rain (acid and other)
Raphael and Other Painters
Rapid Readers
Regional Studies
Reptiles
Research Skills
Research Supplies and Equipment
Revolutions
Rewriting (software)
Russia
Satellites
Satire
Science (anything)
Self-Esteem Programs
Self-Image Programs
Single Parenting
Slide Rules and Other Materials
Somalia
Space Technology
Special Education
Special Needs of Students
State Capitols
State History
Storytelling
Stress in the Family

200 Hot Topics for Grants

Styles of Learning
Student Health Programs of All Kinds
Students in After-School Programs
Success in Reading Programs
Success in Writing Programs
Take-Home Books and Games
Teacher Centers
Teacher Mentoring Programs
Teacher Recruitment
Teaching and Learning in Rural Schools
Technology in the Classroom
Terrariums and Aquariums
Times Tables (software and games)
UFO's and Other Space Phenomena
Ultrasound and Other Medical Marvels
Underachieving Students
Values Education
Violence in Schools
Violent Homes and Families
Water Cycles
Water Pollution
Wellness
Whales and Sharks
Whole Language Materials for Schools
Whole Language Training for Teachers
Winter and Other Seasons (as a theme)
Women's Studies
World Government
World Peace
Writing Across the Curriculum
Writing (school publishing centers)
Writing (software programs)
Writing Workshops for Teachers
Young Children (any project)
Youth and Crime
Youth in Urban Schools
Zeus (mythology in literature and history)
Zoology and Zoo Trips

Fine-Tuning Your Topic and Target

How do you know if your idea is timely and fundable? If the topic did not appear on the list of "200 Hot Topics for Grants," then ask yourself the following questions:

1. Can I locate at least two articles in research journals or popular magazines that discuss my topic? Yes   No
   Examples: *The Reading Teacher* or *Science and Children*

2. Do I know of another grant, based on the same topic, that has recently been awarded? Yes   No
   Grant Title and Funding Source: _____

3. Do I have an overwhelming body of test data or examples of student work or strong case studies that justify the need for this proposal to be funded? Yes   No
   Sources: _____

   _____

   _____

4. If I narrow my idea down a bit, could it fit into one of the "200 Hot Topics for Grants"? For example, a general topic such as "reading" might be narrowed to "reluctant readers." Yes   No

5. My revised topic for the grant is_____.

Now, you can turn to page 44, "Tailor-Made Titles."

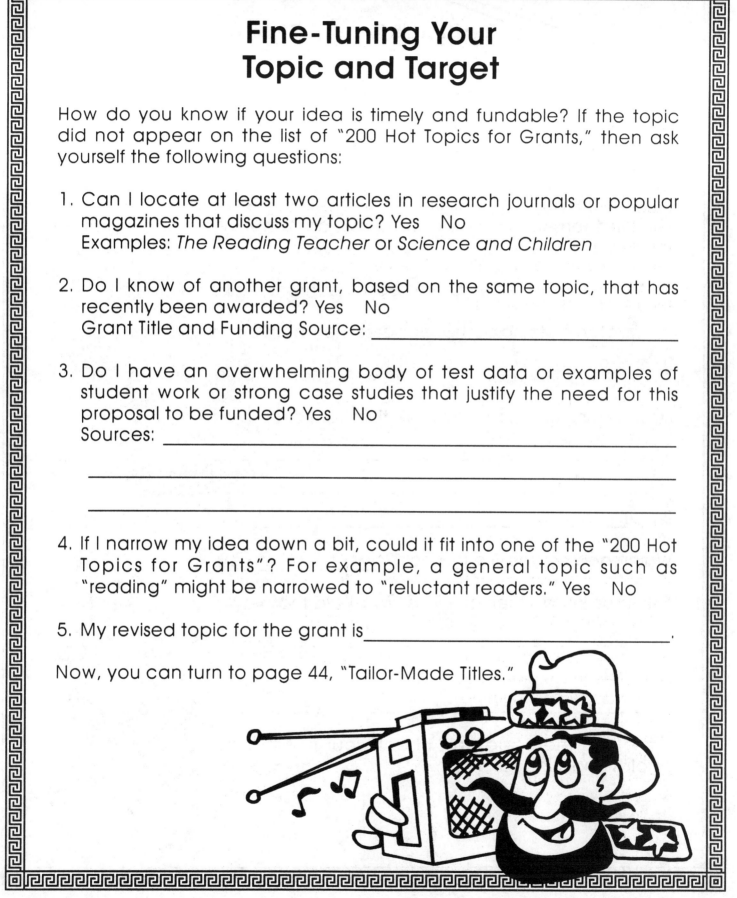

GA1515

Tailor-Made Titles
Tell the Story

Over the years, I have helped over two hundred teachers write original grant proposals. During that time, I found one common link that helped every one of them to focus their writing and to write a stronger proposal. That common link is a catchy, timely, memorable title. When you like your title, chances are the readers will like your title and remember it. A catchy title accomplishes three important things:

1. A catchy title helps you to keep the theme unified.

2. A catchy title helps the reader remember your grant.

3. A catchy title helps you to write the individual sections with flair.

Now, brainstorm a few possible titles for your project.

1. _____

2. _____

3. _____

Which one do you like the best? _____

Ask three others their opinions. What did they say?

_____

_____

_____

Now, turn the page and check your possibilities against the suggestions.

GA1515

Nancy

"Goal-Objectives-Activities...."

How to translate the grant-writing mantra into fundable English

Recently, I caught myself speeding along one of our major interstate highways. I wasn't in a hurry, and I wasn't fleeing some real or imagined threat. I was in a deep, transcendental zone. My foot grew heavier as the hypnotic white lines pulsated before me. I snapped out of it just as my radar detector screeched, warning me of an impending cash outlay and a sentencing to defensive driving school. Suddenly, I shuddered at the thought of those three words that had clouded my consciousness and sent me deep within the abysmal fog. "Goals-objectives-activities," I said, in an expressionless monotone. "Man," I added, "I've been working too hard."

As teachers and administrators, do we know precisely what is meant by these three terms that are the mantra for writing grants? It is difficult enough to stay abreast of changes within our own professions, let alone remain competent in the field of philanthropy and fund solicitation. To many educators either unfamiliar with or intimidated by the grant writing process, the proper use of "goals-objectives-activities" in a proposal is as elusive as the Arctic Yeti.

Goals: Reaching for the heights.

Let's try to unravel the mystery, starting with goals. A goal is many things to many people, but only one thing to a grant funder—what you are trying to achieve, written in very general terms. In a perfect world, all of our goals would be met and surpassed. Because it's not a perfect world, don't lower your expectations. Goals should be constructed just beyond the grasp, requiring extra effort and resources

exceeding normal limits to reach. Kids speak in terms of goals all the time when they say, "I want to be President," or, "I'm going to be an astronaut." Theoretically, there is nothing stopping them from obtaining their goals. Realistically, however, we can assume their chances are slim without strategy and applied effort.

When goals are stated in a grant proposal, they should be lofty. You are looking for a best-case scenario, such as "This project will help students learn telecommunications," or, "Our goal is to make parents more active in homework assignments." As a colleague of mine puts it, "You know something is a goal when, after you say it, optimistic people shout 'Cool!' and pessimistic people shout 'Fat chance!'" Don't worry about measuring your goals—your objectives will do that for you.

Objectives: Down to hard data.

Now let's get our hands dirty and talk about objectives, the meat of every grant proposal, and the part that makes most teachers cringe. There is a simple formula grant applicants can follow when writing objectives, and it is very close to the familiar journalistic code. Objectives must answer who is going to do what, when and where it will be done, and how it will be measured. Recently, I wrote a proposal in which the goal was to effectively deliver adult literacy classes to underserved areas of Indianapolis. The objectives focused on two areas, retention and learning gains, as follows:

Retention: Project REACT staff will accomplish a quarterly 50 percent retention rate for the first year, and a quarterly 50 percent retention rate for

By Dennis M. Norris, the grant writer for the Metropolitan School District in Perry Township, Indianapolis, Ind., and executive director of the Perry Township Education Foundation. Contact him at dnorris@greatlinks.cic.net.

ILLUSTRATION BY CHARLES AKINS

the second year. Rates will be measured comparatively through beginning enrollments, average daily attendance, and average stay in the program.

Learning Gains: For those participants who complete a level of instruction, Project REACT staff will show quarterly group learning gains of 80 percent. Gains will be measured by computer assessment and management programs, use of standardized tests, and evaluation by instructors and tutors on an individualized basis.

As you can see, objectives give real measurement to the pursuit of the goal. They translate lofty ideas into hard data, and they create project benchmarks by which success and/or failure can be gauged.

Activities: Getting busy. Activities can be thought of as the "busywork" of a grant proposal. They indicate how project staff will carry out their tasks in the never-ending quest to meet objectives. Activities are the means to a project's end; they are the nautical chart by which the voyage to objectives is navigated. They may include specific methodology, time lines, testing procedures, logistical strategies, or any number of tasks designed to make the project work.

Activities should be constructed so that they evolve logically from the goals and objectives. That is, to adequately recruit participants to an entry-level adult literacy program, it would not be wise to use text-based brochures and complex registration forms. For Project REACT, activities under the Retention objective included creating computer-generated progress reports, providing professional development for instructors and tutors, and involving members of the community for peer support. To meet the Learning Gains objective, activities centered on adapting testing strategies to participants' learning levels, creating realistic tasks, and modifying student attention span, expectancy, and memory. The activities guided both the physical and

mental tasks of the project, and were the seamless pathway to objective fulfillment and goal attainment.

Remember the mantra. This trio of goals-objectives-activities is truly the mantra of every successful grant writer. One must think in these terms in order to write properly constructed proposals, to impress potential funders, and to

create a usable document that will last the life of the project and beyond. That being said, let's all assume the lotus position, then close your eyes, and repeat after me: "Goals-objectives-activities. Goals-objectives-activities. Goals-objectives-activities. . ." ∎

Tricks for Writing Strong Titles

1. Try an acrostic.
   "Project W.R.E.K."
   "Writing and Reading Engage Kids" is a project to establish a publishing center and classroom library in a third grade classroom.

2. Take off on a movie or book idea.
   "Boys 'n the Library" describes a project to encourage at-risk minority group boys to participate in an after-school reading program.

3. Bandwagon
   "Let's Write!" defines a primary school project aimed at purchasing software for a writing program.

4. Touch the heart.
   "Caring for the Kids" describes an after-school project for latchkey children.

5. Tie into a theme.
   "Project Farm" details a kindergarten teacher's proposal to create an integrated unit on farm life and farm animals that includes a field trip to a local dairy farm.

6. Clue into the curriculum.
   "Science for Daily Living" offers the reader a glimpse of one middle school teacher's proposal to tie daily science experiments into life skills such as measurement and graphing.

7. Please the ear; use alliteration.
   "Reinforcing Reluctant Readers" gives the reader a pleasant introduction to a special education teacher's proposal to give incentives and encouragement to learning disabled middle school students.

Now, make a fresh attempt at a title. Write down your creations.

1. _____

2. _____

3. _____

GA1515

Chapter Review

To wrap up Chapter 3, "Setting the Focus," let's review your progress so far.

1. You feel motivated and confident about your ability to complete a proposal.
   Chapter 1   Yes   No

2. You understand the language of grants and have reviewed the suggested vocabulary.
   Chapter 2   Yes   No

3. You focused on a topic for your proposal and have created a catchy title to pull your proposal together.
   Chapter 3   Yes   No

   My topic is _____

   My topic is _____

4. Now you can proceed to Chapter 4, where you will practice writing a project summary. The project summary is the first section in the narrative. So brew a nice pot of coffee or tea and sharpen your pencils. It is time to do some serious writing.

GA1515

Chapter Four

From Abstract to Ideas

The Narrative

1. The Abstract

2. A Summary or Description

3. Justification

4. Goals and Objectives

5. Matching Evaluation

6. Procedures and Activities

7. Time Line

8. Dissemination

GA1515

Writing Narrative

1. Keep sentences brief.

2. Use the title at least once in each section.

3. Follow the guidelines exactly.

4. Make it look good.

49

Introducing the Letter of Intent

The letter of intent is not necessary if you already have the application packet for your grant. It is applicable, however, when you are approaching an agency or foundation for the first time. The letter of intent is just what it sounds like: a letter informing the grantor that you plan (intend) to submit a full proposal. This letter should contain the following information:

- Your name as the designated project director

- Mailing address of your school and phone number where you can be reached

- School district and grade level of your school

- The kind of grant that you intend to submit
  (Example: a language arts grant for kindergarten)

- The specific funds that you are applying for
  (Example: the Kraft School Innovation Fund)

- A request for an application packet or guidelines

Use this space to practice writing a letter of intent. Check your work against the guidelines from the previous page and compare the final draft with the sample found in Chapter 11.

Letter of Intent Draft

_____

_____

_____

_____

_____

_____

_____

_____

_____

_____

_____

_____

_____

When you are applying for a large grant (an amount over $5000), it is a good practice to submit a letter of intent and an abstract to see if your idea is fundable and of interest to the particular foundation or agency. Experienced grant writers will go a step further and initiate the entire process with a friendly phone call, asking for an application packet and information about deadlines. A sample abstract and letter of intent are included in Chapter 11. But let's take a look at what is expected from a good abstract and letter of intent. Then, we will practice writing each one.

Abstract Absolutes

1. Should be no more than one page in length.

2. Gives a brief overview of the entire project.

3. Offers pertinent information about you and your school.

4. Begins with a statement that will grab the reader's attention and stick in his or her memory.

5. Contains enough details to give a good idea of what your project is about and if it is suited to the foundation or agency that you are approaching.

On the preceding page, we discussed the construction of an abstract. Item #4 on the list referred to a brief opening statement that grabs the reader's attention. What does that mean? How do you accomplish it? Read on.

Abstract Openings

1. A nice quote from a famous educator or author

   "Whole language is an exciting movement in early childhood education, and teachers are making great strides toward reaching a comfortable balance between phonics and whole language instruction in the classroom."   Dr. Linda Bone

2. A startling statistic

   Divorce touches many of the children in our classes. In fact, over 50 percent of elementary students will experience serious disruptions in their home situations.

3. A rhetorical question

   What is the best way to help children gain confidence in their ability to succeed in school?

4. A statement from a new, important piece of research

   A 1993 study released by the American Association of University Women reveals that sexual harassment of boys and girls begins during the elementary school years.

5. A brief, personal anecdote that is either humorous or touching

   I have never thought much about the importance of providing a snack during kindergarten until I met Mario. This bright little five-year-old enters my classroom eager to learn and eager to eat. Our ten o'clock snack is his first meal of the day.

Attempting an Abstract

Use this page to practice writing a one-page abstract for your grant. Use the guidelines offered on the previous page and compare your attempt with the sample abstract found in Chapter 12.

Abstract for _____

(title of project)

_____

_____

_____

_____

_____

_____

_____

_____

_____

_____

_____

_____

_____

_____

_____

_____

_____

_____

_____

_____

_____

WHO WHAT WHEN WHERE HOW

With your title and topic in hand, you are ready for the first phase of the narrative. This is called the Project Summary, or in some cases, the Project Description. This is not the same as an abstract, which we will tackle in the next few pages.

In writing the summary, you need to respond to these questions:

Who will be served by my project?
(the client group)

How long will the project take?
(duration)

What is the problem area addressed by my proposal and why is it important?
(justification and goal statement)

What kinds of activities will be used to solve the problem?
(project)

How will we know if the project is successful?
(evaluation)

Using the questions outlined on the previous page, let's practice writing a summary. Use words from the "Choose the Right Word" list to make your writing exciting, and follow the first two rules of writing narrative.

Rule One: Keep your sentences brief.

Rule Two: Use the title of your project at least once in each section.

Now use this space to write a summary of your project. You can compare your summary with the sample grant found in Chapter 12 of the book.

Summary of _____
(title of your grant)

_____

_____

_____

_____

_____

_____

_____

_____

_____

_____

_____

GA1515

(cont'd.)

Chapter Review

Let's review what you have learned about moving from "Abstract to Ideas" before you go into Chapter 5. Did you do the following:

1. Include the who, what, when, and why information?   Yes   No

2. Check your summary against the sample in Chapter 12?
   Yes   No

3. Check your summary against the guidelines set in the application packet for your specific grant proposal, if you have them?
   Yes   No

4. Follow the first two rules for writing narrative?   Yes   No

Before we move on to the next chapter, let's go over the rules for writing narrative, and add a third one:

Rule One: Keep your sentences brief.

Rule Two: Use the title of your project at least once in each section.

Rule Three: Follow the guidelines for content and format that are set down in the application packet. Do not deviate from them, even if they are not consistent with those set out in this book. Every agency has its own rules, and they will be judging your proposal, not this writer.

Proceed to Chapter 5.

GA1515

Justification: Why Should We Fund You?

Welcome to Chapter 5. If I had to name the most important chapter in *Grant Writing for Teachers*, this would be it. This is the longest and most detailed chapter. This is your opportunity to do the following:

1. Explain the rationale for your proposal.
2. State the reasons why your proposal is important.
3. Convince the readers of the importance and impact of your grant.
4. Justify your request for funds.
5. Defend your proposal's value.
6. Confirm the need for a program such as the one you propose.
7. Present data and studies that uphold the need for your project.
8. Affirm your project by presenting letters of support.
9. Legitimize your proposal by linking it to current research.
10. Seek approval for your project by defining critical need and substantial problem area.

GA1515

Your guidelines may call this section one of the following:

1. Problem area
2. Justification
3. Statement of the problem
4. Needs assessment
5. Rationale for funding
6. Defense of the proposal
7. Summary of the problem

Whatever the jargon is, this is your opportunity to make your case for funding. This is critical. I recommend that you outline your defense in four paragraphs or sections. The following pages will give you a full description of what should be included in each section. For now, here is the outline.

Paragraph One: Client group and description of the setting and scope of the problem

Paragraph Two: Description of supporting data including both qualitative and quantitative data

Paragraph Three: Link your proposal to current research.

Paragraph Four: Strengthen your case with expert support.

Turn the page to begin formulating the first paragraph or section. Remember to use the title of your grant in each of the four paragraphs when you write the draft.

GA1515

Section One: Justification

Objective: The grant writer will describe the nature of the problem area and the reason for the problem.

Objective: The grant writer will describe the setting of the school and community in which the problem occurs.

Objective: The grant writer will describe the group of students affected by the problem and the teachers or other professionals who will intervene.

In the first section of the justification, you must include all of the information that was cited above. Let's consider your proposal.

Question One: How would you describe your problem? Can you be specific and avoid jargon? What are the reasons for the problem? Look at the list of "problems" that follows. Put an X by the ones that are not specific enough to be included in an explanation.

☐ A ten-point drop in reading comprehension scores in the past two years

☐ Too much violence in schools

☐ Over two thirds of the kindergarten students are eligible for free or reduced lunch.

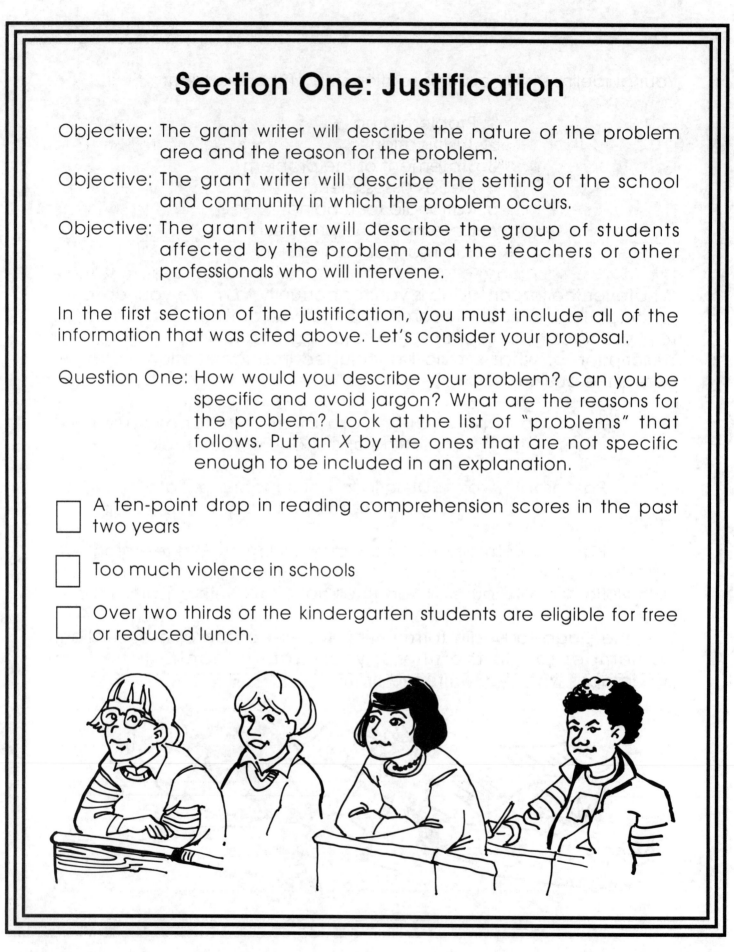

☐ Our library has been put on "probation" because the collection is outdated.

☐ More than twenty-five incidents of child abuse are reported in our school each quarter.

☐ The use of computers in our labs has decreased by fifteen hours per week during the last year.

☐ More children have signed up for the after-school program than we have spaces for.

☐ Too many children are left alone after school.

☐ Mathematics scores increase by 10 percent when students have access to manipulatives during the first and second grades.

☐ Science scores are too low in America.

How many Xs did you mark? The correct answer is 3!

Now, describe the nature of the problem that your proposal addresses and include a brief rationale for that problem. Use specific information and avoid broad generalizations.

_____

_____

_____

_____

_____

_____

_____

GA1515

Here's how one teacher described her problem area:

During the past three years, the number of five-year-olds who enter our kindergarten program "not ready" for school, based on the DIAL-R test, has increased by 20 percent. Meanwhile, our class size has also increased, while the number of teaching assistants has decreased. We need help in providing more one-on-one instruction for these children if they are going to have a successful kindergarten experience.

• Note the specific nature of the problem area.
• Note the details provided that "paint a picture."

Stating the problem is important, but it must be put within the context of "setting." Now think about this question: "Why is your particular school unique? How does the setting of your school's community relate to the problem? This next exercise will help to focus.

Circle the phrases that might describe your school or community.

low-income   influx of refugees or immigrants

high unemployment rate   large group of latchkey children

high transition rate   impacted by military

inner city   ethnically diverse

an overcrowded school   low tax base

a farming community   rural

many single parent families

high population of non-English speaking children

When describing your problem, the setting can and does add to the scope of the issue. Be specific and describe how and why the geographic, socioeconomic, and cultural attributes of your school and community make it especially needy.

Here is an example of how one school described its unique situation and its audience.

Pineville Elementary School is a small (300 students in grades k-4), rural school located in the western corner of Blaine County. The school has never been especially wealthy, but has recently been drained by a series of lay-offs at the Blaine County Lumber Mill, the largest local employer. The county will be unable to supplement our library renovation and we are seeking private funding for Project Read to Me, in order to build up the collection and to add three new Apple Computers to the technology resource center in the library.

Now you describe your school setting. _____

_____

_____

_____

_____

- Notice how the name of the school and school population are given.
- Notice how the title of the grant is worked in.
- Notice how the narrative "paints a picture" of the setting.
- Notice how the "intervention" is woven into the last sentence? This tells how the problem can be addressed.

Justification has four important sections. These may be long paragraphs. Here are the key points of the second paragraph.

1. Quantitative data
2. Qualitative data

To be most convincing and effective, give the reader examples of both kinds of data to show how needy your students are and how important your project will be.

Now you are thinking, "What do you mean by quantitative and qualitative data?" Let me give you some examples.

Quantitative Data

Give a summary of scores from standardized tests. Show percentages from demographic data or census data. Use a bar graph showing a decline in attendance or an increase in school violence. Use IQ scores or other validated tests. Display a school profile from achievement tests.

Important Hint: Always use the National Percentiles from tests—they will usually be far lower than your local scores and will demonstrate a greater need.

Qualitative Data

Summarize anecdotal records of student behavior. Use the results of a parent or teacher questionnaire. Survey students' attitudes with an "Attitude Inventory." Give examples from student interviews or journals. Take data from behavior check-lists. Use a mini case study to document student need. Give examples of work from portfolios of student work. Create a teacher-made test to assess a level of content knowledge or achievement.

GA1515

In the third section of the project justification, fortify your position by linking the problem with current research in the field. This demonstrates the validity and severity of the problem area. Here are some examples of how this connection works.

Research Connections

Grant Topic	Support
Children's literature	*The Reading Teacher*
Preschool children	*Young Children*
	Lollipops magazine
Math	National Council of Teachers of Mathematics publications
Curriculum design or change	*Curriculum Review*
	Educational Leadership
	The Kappan
Families	*Journal of Marriage and the Family*
	Parents Magazine
	Growing Parent
Teaching innovations	*Instructor*
	Pre-K Today
	The NEW Good Apple Newspaper
	Educational Oasis
Gifted education	*Challenge*
	Gifted Child Today
	Gifted Child Quarterly
General education	*Education Today*
	Education Digest
Special education	Journals of the Council for Exceptional Children

GA1515

Keep in mind that the journals and magazines mentioned on the previous page are simply a start. You can look for support in *Time, Newsweek, Psychology Today*, and even *The Wall Street Journal*. These publications often run articles about important trends in education.

The local newspaper is also a good source. Keep a file of articles that mention major research studies that have been released. You can then follow up later and request information from the specific organization. A good source for data on families is the *Kids Count Data Book*, which is available from the Ann Casey Foundation.

Talk with your school librarian or call a local university to find out about the availability of journals. It is a good idea to do an "Eric Search" or "Info-Trac" search to find out what has been recently published in your area of interest.

Your goal is to use the research to write a short paragraph explaining why your proposal is timely and important. You cite the article, author, and a few facts from the article in the narrative and then attach the article or clipping as an addendum to the grant. See the following page for an example of how this works.

Finish up your justification section by mentioning a letter of support from a local expert such as a college professor, medical doctor, counselor, PTA president, or member of a professional organization. In the final paragraph, you cite the letter of support and mention a few points from the letter, and then attach the actual letter as an addendum. This is a final touch that demonstrates how vital and needed your project is.

Example: Research Connection

The need for Project Read to Me can be documented in the current research. In the May 1993 issue of *The Reading Teacher*, Dr. Mary Smythe reports that school libraries play a significant role in encouraging reading for pleasure. The September 1992 issue of *Lollipops* lists important new books for young children, and none of these books are currently available in our library because of funding cuts. Project Read to Me would help the Pineville Library to meet the needs of its students by updating the holdings and by providing more programs for children and families. (See Addenda II and III, articles.)

Example: Letter of Support

Finally, the importance of Project Read to Me can be underscored by a letter of support from Dr. Mike Jones, professor of Education at Pineville College. Dr. Jones states, "The Pineville Elementary Library needs support to continue its commitment to young children. Reading for pleasure and research reading are both essential in the school experience, and the grant would enable this school to make great strides in both areas." Dr. Jones' entire letter is included as an addendum to the proposal. (See Addendum V.)

You have learned about these four areas that should be covered in your justification:

1. How and why of the problem
2. The setting and audience
3. Current research in the problem area
4. Local support for the problem

It is sometimes compelling to mention your own background and unique qualifications to implement the project, if you have a good bit of teaching experience or have implemented similar projects. You can do this in part 2 or 4 and attach your résumé as an addendum.

Before you work on a draft of areas 3 and 4, respond to the following items:

1. List at least two research or teaching journals that might contain articles to support the proposal.

_____   _____

2. List at least two "experts" that could be called on to write a letter of support for the proposal.

_____   _____

Draft of Sections 3 and 4

_____

_____

_____

_____

GA1515

_____

_____

_____

_____

_____

_____

_____

****

Reminders

1. Did you follow the four rules for writing narrative?
2. Did you label articles and letters as addenda?
3. Did you choose lively words from the list in Chapter 2?
4. Did you link the four sections with transition words from the Chapter 2 list?
5. Does your draft sound convincing?

****

Sometimes a teacher needs to create a special kind of justification to demonstrate the unique nature of the problem area that he or she is attacking. Teacher-made assessments and inventories can be helpful. Turn the page to see an example of this kind of instrument.

Creating Your Own Data

Sometimes it is difficult to find enough "hard evidence" in the form of test scores or even existing surveys or demographic data to complete the second section of your justification. That's okay. Teachers are famous for "making do." In grant writing, teachers can effectively make and take data on their own. Here is an example of how this works.

The Problem

Meg Jones is a kindergarten teacher who wants to write a grant to purchase outdoor play equipment and riding toys for her students who live in an inner-city housing project. She believes that the children's gross motor skills would improve if these activities were available at school. She also thinks that the physical activity would make them more alert and ready to learn. How can she document such information?

The Response

Meg Jones can create her own behavior checklist and administer it as a pre- and posttest. The pretest data will probably show that the children can master only a limited number of tasks. She can use the same instrument in the evaluation section of the grant as one way to measure the success of the grant.

The Golden Rule of Creating Instruments

The Meg Jones scenario illustrates what I call the "Golden Rule of Creating Instruments." Get double mileage out of the checklists, pre- and posttests, behavior inventories, or rating scales that you design. Use them in two ways:

First, to show a need;
Second, as an evaluation tool.

72

Sample Behavior Checklist

Directions: List each student and rate his or her ability level in each of the cognitive, social, and psychomotor tasks.

The key for this checklist is:

* strength   + acceptable   x weakness

Teacher _____ School _____

Date of Assessment _____ Purpose _____

	Name	Chronological Age	Task	Rating
1.				
2.				
3.				
4.				
5.				
6.				
7.				
8.				
9.				
10.				
11.				
12.				
13.				
14.				
15.				
16.				
17.				

Chapter Review

Congratulations! You have completed Chapter 5, the longest and toughest chapter in the book. How do you feel? Have you made a strong case for your proposal? In order to leave no stone unturned, let's review your justification knowledge and skills.

****

Did you state the problem clearly and with a conversational, not scientific tone?   Yes   No

Did you have both qualitative and quantitative data to support the proposal?   Yes   No

Did you discuss at least one important study or article that is related to your problem?   Yes   No

Did you attach and mention a strong letter of support?   Yes   No

Did you create a versatile test or instrument that can be used for need and for evaluation later on?   Yes   No

Did you use any addenda and if so, did you label them and highlight the important phrases?   Yes   No

Does your justification section show four clean paragraphs that are linked by transition words and mention the title of the grant at least once?   Yes   No

****

You are ready to proceed to Chapter 6: Goals and Objectives.

Chapter Six

$$$$$ $$$$$

Goals and Objectives

75

GA1515

Getting to the Goal

After you have given the reader a brief introduction to the project through the project summary or description, it is time to get down to specifics. Most guidelines ask you to make a "broad statement" about the intent or direction of the grant. This is called a goal. Keep in mind, the goal is not the same as an objective. That section is next.

Let's look at a few sample goal statements, and then you can practice writing them as well.

Sample One: The goal of **Project WET** is to introduce young children to the abundance of wildlife and marine resources in their local marsh areas.

Sample Two: The goal of **Project "Let's Eat"** is to offer middle school students the opportunity to learn about supply and demand in business while operating a school concession stand.

Sample Three: The goal of **Project Math Magic** is to provide manipulatives and a part-time curriculum expert for regular classroom teachers.

Sample Four: The goal of **Project LIFT (Learning Is For Teachers)** is to offer teachers in rural schools the opportunity to learn new methods for teaching geography and history.

GA1515

Notice That:

1. The project title is stated and is highlighted by underlining or boldface or quotation marks. Choose one method and apply it consistently!

2. Words such as *learn* and *understand* are acceptable here but never in an objective.

3. Goals talk about the project outcomes while objectives will discuss learner outcomes.

4. The goal is a broad, sweeping statement. You do not provide times, dates, or criteria for success.

Practice Writing Three Sample Goal Statements

1. The goal of Project _____ is to _____

_____

_____

_____

2. The goal of Project _____ is to _____

_____

_____

_____

3. The goal of Project _____ is to _____

_____

_____

_____

GA1515

The Object Is to Write Clear Objectives

One of the most frequently cited weaknesses in grant proposals is poorly written objectives. Objectives often suffer from one or more of the following faults:

- Not measurable
- Not written in terms of learner outcome
- Too long
- Unrealistic and unmatched to evaluation
- Missing important information

Now that you have looked at what might weaken an objective, let's go over the essential components of an objective and write some examples.

Objectives Must:

1. Be written with a measurable action verb. Never use *learn* or *understand*. (See Chapter 2 for a list of verbs.)

   Correct: The students will complete six original books during the project period.

   Incorrect: The students will learn to write books.

2. Use a learner outcome format.

   Correct: The students will complete six original books during the project period.

   Incorrect: The grant will consist of writing original books.

GA1515

3. Be brief and clear.

    Correct: The students will complete six original books during the project period.

    Incorrect: The talented young people will write, illustrate, bind, and print six exciting books during their unique opportunity for publishing offered by my grant.

4. Match every objective with a realistic outcome or evaluation criterion.

    Correct Match and Realistic:

    Objective One: The students will complete six original books during the project period.

    Outcome One: During the school year 1993-94, the six original books will be collected in a portfolio and will be evaluated using the First Grade Writing Checklist. (Addendum II)

    Incorrect Match and Unrealistic:

    Objective One: The students will complete six original books during the project period.

    Outcome One: By the end of the project year, reading scores for the entire first grade will increase by 20 percent.

5. Include information on what will occur and who will do the learning or doing.

    Correct: The students will complete six original books during the project year.

    Incorrect: The students will write books.

GA1515

Before You Practice Writing Objectives, Here Is Another Hint: The fewer objectives, the better. In small grants (those under $5000), I tell teachers to stick to three good objectives and to match them with three strong outcomes. That makes for a better project. Do a few things well and measure them well, and you will have a stronger case for funding. Now let's write.

Objective One: _____

_____

_____

_____

Objective Two: _____

_____

_____

_____

Objective Three: _____

_____

_____

_____

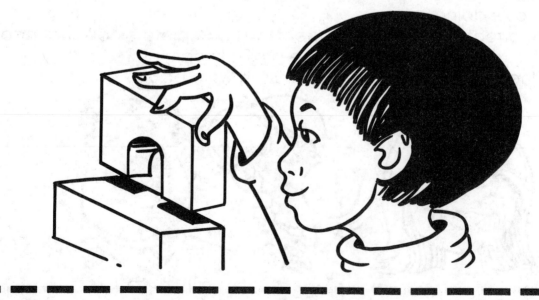

80

Making the Most of Your Objectives

Now that you have practiced writing objectives, let's take a look at how to present those objectives effectively. In writing narrative, there is a fourth rule to remember: Make it look good and sound good.

The format and appearance of your narrative will have almost as much impact as the words themselves. So, do the following with your objectives:

1. Present objectives and evaluation in a numbered list and double-space between items.

2. Introduce the objectives with one of the following phrases, then follow with the numbered items:

As a result of Project _____, we anticipate the following outcomes:

    1. _____

    2. _____

Through Project _____, we plan to attain the following:

    1. _____

    2. _____

The funding of Project _____ will result in the following:

    1. _____

    2. _____

GA1515

Chapter Review

At this point, you have written three sections of the narrative, or written portion of the proposal. The budget, you recall, is the second portion of the proposal. So far, you have completed the following:

1. A summary or description
2. Problem area or justification
3. Goals and objectives

Let's review the criteria for goals and objectives.

1. Is your goal a broad statement about the project?   Yes   No

2. You can have up to three goals. How many do you have? _____

3. Objectives should be specific and measurable. List only the verbs that are in your objectives:

   _____ _____ _____

4. Did you use the title of your project in this section?   Yes   No

   How did you highlight the title? _____

5. Did you plan for a matching evaluation for every objective?
   Yes   No

Now you may proceed to Chapter 7 and evaluation.

GA1515

Evaluation

Chapter Seven

GA1515

Evaluation: The Weak Link in Proposals

When a foundation or government agency gives your school money to solve a problem or to research a solution, the question in everyone's mind is: "Did it work?"

That makes sense. People want to know if their investment paid off. Evaluation gives them that payoff. Evaluation should be designed to answer these questions:

****

1. Did you meet the objectives that were set?
2. To what degree were you successful in meeting the goals and objectives?
3. How did you document the outcomes of the project?
4. How did you present the data that illustrates the outcome of the project?

****

Evaluation is often called the "weak link" in grants, because so few writers actually design a cogent, rational plan for measuring and reporting the results of the project.

You can be different. You can make your evaluation section tight, neat, and clear. And by doing so, you can bring home the dollars.

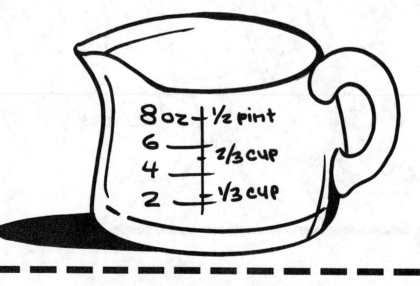

Excellent Evaluations

When you write the evaluation plan, keep in mind the major weakness that readers point to: inadequate evaluation. Why inadequate?

- The evaluation criteria do not match one-to-one with the objectives.
- The evaluation plan does not give a criterion or percentage or goal that indicates success.
- The evaluation plan does not detail the instruments, checklists, tests, or procedures that will be used to report project outcomes.
- The evaluation plan is not realistic. It is too complex or expensive or has set expectations that are unbelievable.

****

Make your evaluation plan more than adequate. Make it something that you can actually use to assess the project and to collect data that will help you to secure even more funding. Plan the evaluation around these guidelines:

- Follow the four rules for writing narrative.
- Use measurable, short words and brief sentences.
- Attach copies of the instruments that you will use as assessment or to report data. Mark these as Addenda.
- Match your evaluation one-to-one with objectives.
- Give the percentage or score or participation level that you desire for a successful project.
- Keep your evaluation plan simple and realistic.

Make the Evaluation Plan Look Good

Remember the old adage "You can't tell a book by the cover"? Well don't apply that philosophy to grant writing. It will get you into trouble. Grants have to look sharp. Format counts. Procedures and order matter. Keep that in mind while writing the evaluation plan. Use this format:

****

The evaluation plan for **Project Read to Me** includes the following outcomes:

Evaluation One: By the end of the project year, 1994, all of the participating students will read at least twenty-five library books from their appropriate reading levels. The reading will be documented by the teacher-made **Read to Me** checklist. (Addendum I: copy of checklist)

Evaluation Two: By the end of the project year, 1994, all of the participating students will demonstrate an increase of at least 3 percentage points on the reading comprehension subtest of the Metropolitan Reading Test. This will be documented using the Class Profile Sheet. (Addendum II: copy of Profile Sheet)

Evaluation Three: By the end of the project year, 1994, at least 85 percent of the families surveyed will report an increase in the time that is spent reading aloud to children. The **Read to Me** Parent Questionnaire will be used to assess this change. (Addendum III: copy of questionnaire)

****

Now that you have the format down, take a practice run at writing some evaluation.

Draft of Evaluation for Project _____

The evaluation plan for Project _____
includes the following outcomes:

Evaluation One: _____

_____

_____

_____

_____

Evaluation Two: _____

_____

_____

_____

_____

Evaluation Three: _____

_____

_____

_____

_____

GA1515

Questions and Answers About Evaluation

Question: How many evaluation criteria does it take to make the plan work?

Answer: You need one evaluation for every one objective.

Question: How do you document intangibles such as an increase in self-esteem or greater student interest in schoolwork?

Answer: You can design an original questionnaire or attitude inventory and give it in a pre-post method to show a change. You can also use the interview method or student journals, but these should only supplement some sort of instrument. A sample attitude inventory is given in this section.

Question: What about standardized tests as evaluation? I thought they were losing ground in favor of alternative forms of assessment.

Answer: Yes and no. Standardized tests have been sharply criticized in recent years, but they can still be effective as evaluation, if you balance them with alternatives, such as gathering portfolios of student work.

Question: I like the idea of portfolios. Is it adequate to say that you will simply keep a portfolio of each student's work?

Answer: No. You would lose points for incomplete evaluation. When using the portfolio method, you need to design a checklist of what will be included in the portfolio and some sample criteria for evaluating that work.

Question: Shouldn't you set high goals in the evaluation section? Won't that make your proposal look ambitious?

Answer: It might make you look ridiculous. Set strong, yet attainable goals in your evaluation section, and you will be competitive. For example, you might anticipate a 5-point increase in mathematics scores for each student rather than saying that every student will score above the 90th percentile on the mathematics test.

Question: I wrote a proposal that was turned down because the evaluation did not measure the objectives. What did that mean?

Answer:  You might have followed the format, but the evaluation was not valid. That means it didn't measure what it was supposed to measure. For example: In a grant about geography, don't use a general achievement test to measure the outcome. You need a content-based geography test. Attach a copy of the test, too, so the readers will not have to guess at the validity of the test.

Question: How do you spell success? Is it the same in every evaluation plan? Does it always means the same thing?

Answer:  Certainly not. Your evaluation plan will reflect the complexity of the problem that you are addressing. In some schools, it is unrealistic to expect 100 percent parent participation in a family math project. So set your criterion accordingly and link it to earlier statements made in the Justification.

Question: What about attaching addenda? Does anybody really look at them? Can you attach too many?

Answer: The answer is that addenda can be helpful in showing the validity of your evaluation. When you mention a teacher-made assessment, the reader needs an opportunity to look at it. Yes, readers look at addenda. Yes, you can attach too much. That is why you plan for just three objectives and matching evaluation.

Empower Yourself with Evaluation

Remember the "A + B = C" formula for writing grants? Well, it is clearly applicable in designing evaluation. When you plan a lesson, you plan for assessment . . . right? As a professional, you are concerned with the outcome in terms of student learning. As a caring individual, you are concerned with the student's affective and social behaviors. So, you plan for ways to answer the question: "Did it work?" In grant writing, we look for creative, cogent ways to respond to that same question. Here are some ideas for designing an evaluation plan for your grant, without reinventing the wheel.

1. Adopt a sample assessment from a Good Apple resource book such as *Creative, Hands-On Science Experiences* (GA165), by Dr. Jerry DeBruin. This book contains several nice sample instruments that could be used for evaluation in a science or social studies grant.

2. Look through back issues of *Weekly Reader* and *Scholastic* magazines for content area tests in areas such as geography and civics.

3. Ask resource teachers in speech, music, art, guidance, and physical education to provide an assessment technique or instrument that might be appropriate for your classroom project.

4. Design a matrix using skills and behaviors that will be covered in your procedures and then mark out boxes in the matrix as students complete the tasks.

GA1515

5. Try an evaluation technique in which the students keep up with their own progress. For example, in a "Green Thumb" proposal that I once wrote, second graders literally dipped their thumbs in a green ink pad and marked off the skills on their Skill Chart. The grant involved a unit on plant life and provided funds to build a greenhouse at the school. This technique could also be used in any kind of language arts or publishing center grant. Kids would use a black ink pad to make a mark on the skills chart. How about blue ink for a marine life grant? Do you get the idea?

6. Consider bringing in an outside evaluator or even a team of evaluators from another school to observe and write an evaluation for your project. This is especially advisable in large grants (over $10,000).

7. Apply the "golden rule" in designing evaluation: If you created a nice test or instrument to prove that there was a need (justification) for your project, then turn around and use that same instrument to evaluate the project.

8. Name your original instrument and make it look professional. One creative principal that I worked with designed a one-page Citizenship Behavior Inventory that was referred to as the CBI. This nifty little instrument was crucial in helping him secure funding three years in a row for his citizenship grant.

9. Don't be afraid to use a school-wide standardized test as part of your evaluation plan, if there is an appropriate subtest that fits your plan. For example, a subtest in the area of problem solving is appropriate for many science and math grants.

10. If you are a special education teacher or if you have special students who are mainstreamed into your class, plan to use the IEP (Individualized Education Plan) as part of your evaluation.

91

GA1515

Sample Attitude Inventory for _____
                                          (Project Title)

1. I feel confident about my ability to_____.
   Always   Sometimes   Never

2. I enjoy working on _____ projects with others.
   Always   Sometimes   Never

3. I would rate myself as this kind of student in _____.
   Strong   Average   Weak

4. I look forward to coming to school every day.
   Usually   Sometimes   Seldom

5. _____is my favorite subject.
         Yes   No   I don't know.

6. These three words describe my feelings about _____.
   _____   _____   _____

7. I think _____ is helping me to become a problem solver.
         Yes   No   I don't know.

8. Learning about _____ makes me feel interested.
         Often   Sometimes   Seldom

9. _____ is too hard for me to learn.
         Yes   No   I don't know.

10. I feel good about what I am doing in _____.
         Often   Sometimes   Seldom

Chapter Review

Evaluation is often called the _____ in the chain of grant writing. How did you fill in that blank? Is it the vulnerable point in your narrative? It need not be if you followed the suggestions on pages 90-91. To check yourself, respond to these true or false items.

1. You must match objectives and evaluations.   True   False

2. Standardized tests can never be used in an evaluation plan.   True   False

3. It is not a good idea to have students keep up with their own progress as part of the evaluation plan.   True   False

4. You must create an original instrument if you want your project to be funded.   True   False

5. It is not necessary to name your instrument. Just call it checklist or test.   True   False

6. Evaluation must be complex to be effective.   True   False

7. You don't always have to set a criterion in evaluation.   True   False

8. It is acceptable to have more evaluation than you do objectives.   True   False

****

Items one and eight are true. The rest are false. You can have more than one way to evaluate a single objective as long as you have at least one match.

GA1515

Chapter Eight

Activities and Procedures

Welcome to Chapter 8: Activities and Procedures. In the "A + B = C" method for grant writing, this is the part that most closely resembles lesson planning. If you have made it this far, relax. The rest is a piece of cake!

Building on the case that you made with a lively summary, a powerful justification, detailed objectives, and a careful evaluation plan, you can now simply tell your readers exactly what you want to.

This section is about procedures, activities, or in some grants, methods. Whatever the word, the practice is the same. You must clearly and completely spell out:

• What you plan to do
• How you will use materials and equipment purchased with grant funds
• How long it will take (time line)
• How personnel will be used in the activities
• How you will disseminate your project
• And most importantly, how you will correlate these procedures with goals and objectives

Planning for Perfect Procedures

Step One: Organize

Write your procedures in small blocks or sections that are unified by a common theme. For example:
- Procedures for identifying students
- Activities that students will be involved in
- Procedures for ordering materials
- Activities that parents will be involved in
- Procedures for training of personnel
- Methods for disseminating information about the grant
- Dates and activities on the time line

Sample Activities Section

Project Let's Read will be implemented through the following student activities:

1. A master storyteller, Ron Jones, will visit the school twice each month to perform for students in grades k-4.

2. Students will participate in a reading incentive program that will include rewards of book bags and T-shirts as they meet individual target goals.

3. A school-wide publishing center will be set up in the library so that students can write, illustrate, and bind their own books in one place.

4. Children's author Mary Smythe will visit the school during Children's Book Week to read from her new book, *Bears Forever*, and to participate in a workshop for teachers and an autograph party for parents and children.

Pointers on Procedures

Did you notice that the sample activities and procedures:

- Gave specific names and approximate times whenever possible? You want to "flesh out" your activities with specifics.
- Were brief and not too wordy? Procedures need to be clear and yet direct. Use active words from Chapter 2 in this section.
- Made realistic and cost-effective claims? A children's author visits during Children's Book Week, not every month. That would be realistic.

Practice Writing Procedures

Project_____will be implemented through the following procedures and activities:

Block One:_____(Area)
Be sure to number each procedure and follow the four rules for writing narrative.

_____

_____

_____

_____

_____

_____

_____

_____

GA1515

Block Two: _____ (area)

_____

_____

_____

_____

_____

Block Three: _____ (area)

_____

_____

_____

_____

_____

Block Four: _____ (area)

_____

_____

_____

_____

_____

Tips for a Terrific Time Line

As you complete the procedures section, you will be required to draw up a simple yet important plan for completing your activities according to a set schedule. This is called a **time line**. The time line should be chronological, orderly, and thorough. Be sure to include target dates for:

- Ordering materials and equipment
- Giving pre- and posttests
- Identifying participants
- Training personnel
- Beginning and completing the project
- Site visits (if applicable)
- Completing evaluation
- Project dissemination
- Follow-up and research
- Important field trips and speakers
- Grading periods and standardized test dates if they are part of your evaluation plan
- An overall calendar of events related to project objectives

GA1515

Practice Time Line for Project _____

January _____ (year)

_____

_____

_____

February _____ (year)

_____

_____

_____

March _____ (year)

_____

_____

_____

April _____ (year)

_____

_____

_____

May _____ (year)

_____

_____

_____

June _____ (year)

_____

_____

_____

GA1515

July _____ (year)

_____

_____

_____

August _____ (year)

_____

_____

_____

September _____ (year)

_____

_____

_____

October _____ (year)

_____

_____

_____

November _____ (year)

_____

_____

_____

December _____ (year)

_____

_____

_____

Time Line Extended for Follow-Up and Dissemination

_____

_____

_____

GA1515

Dissemination: The Final Procedure

The final step in writing procedures is to describe your method of dissemination. This refers to your plan for sharing and spreading the ideas generated by your grant. Foundations and government think tanks put a great deal of emphasis on dissemination. The idea is that their investment (your grant) should yield high interest (dissemination). They want other schools and communities to learn from your efforts and to apply practices and procedures in their own settings. The question now is this: "What makes a strong dissemination plan?"

103

GA1515

Dissemination Dos and Don'ts

The Dos

Be creative.

Present at conferences and workshops.

Use newsletters and professional journals to disseminate ideas.

Use technology such as audio- and videotapes to spread your ideas.

Develop an exportable product that can be inexpensively repro- duced and shared with many teachers.

The Don'ts

Plan to present at one hundred sites.

Rely solely on written methods.

Plan for an expensive technology-based plan that you cannot be successful in.

Develop an exportable product that is trite and shoddy. It will reduce the polish and impact of your plan.

Brainstorm eight innovative ideas for disseminating your project.

1. _____

2. _____

3. _____

4. _____

5. _____

6. _____

7. _____

8. _____

GA1515

Pitfalls in Procedures

Unrealistic Plans

Too Rich for Budget

Weak Dissemination

Sketchy Time Line

No Correlation to Objectives

Boring Activities

GA1515

Chapter Review

How did you like writing procedures? It was a lot like writing a lesson plan, wasn't it? Now you have completed the toughest part of the grant, the narrative. Putting together a budget isn't hard. Everyone enjoys spending money, especially someone else's money! Before you move into Chapter 9, take a moment to review what you have learned about writing procedures.

****

Directions: Rewrite each statement so that it is correct.

1. Activities can be broad and general. It is not important to give specific titles, dates, and personnel.

   _____

2. The time line does not require information about training and dissemination.

   _____

3. Dream a little bit in your plan for dissemination. Nobody expects you to actually accomplish it.

   _____

4. Procedures, activities, and method usually mean three different things.

   _____

GA1515

Chapter Nine

Budget Details

GA1515

No matter how large or small your grant may be, it will have two parts: a narrative and a budget. We have devoted eight chapters to designing and writing narrative, and now we will turn our attention to budget. This is relatively simple, so just one chapter will take care of the deed. Everyone enjoys spending money, right? But did you know that there is a technique for spending money appropriately? In grant design, there are ten rules for budgeting.

****

Ten Rules for Budgeting Grant Dollars

1. Design a budget that is realistic, not too cheap nor too fancy.

2. Design a budget that covers every objective.

3. Itemize everything.

4. Stick to whole dollar amounts.

5. Show as much outside contribution as possible, both in real dollars and in-kind.

6. Make sure that the budget follows the time line.

7. Plan for contingencies and emergencies. This shows responsibility.

8. Keep personnel costs reasonable and give a basis for each salary.

9. Avoid waste.

10. Be cautious about big-ticket items such as computers and office equipment. They make a budget look top-heavy.

GA1515

Budget Breakdown

Use these categories to brainstorm all the possible items or services that you might need for your proposal. Then, in the next section, itemize these same items in order of priority. Finally, select items from each category until you have met your target amount.

****

Wish List

Equipment	Cost per Item	Projected Total
_____	_____	_____
_____	_____	_____
_____	_____	_____
_____	_____	_____
_____	_____	_____
_____	_____	_____
_____	_____	_____

Supplies	Cost per Item	Projected Total
_____	_____	_____
_____	_____	_____
_____	_____	_____
_____	_____	_____
_____	_____	_____
_____	_____	_____

GA1515

Purchased Services (field trips, fees, honoraria)

_____

_____

_____

_____

Personnel: Salaries and Benefits
List the title of each person and the projected salary.

_____   _____

_____   _____

_____   _____

_____   _____

Audiovisual, Software, Books, Curriculum Materials
List title, publisher, and price per item.

_____

_____

_____

_____

_____

Training of Staff

_____

_____

_____

Postage, Long Distance Phone Calls

_____

_____

_____

Dissemination Plan

_____

_____

_____

Refreshments and Supplies for Meetings, Workshops, etc.

_____

_____

_____

Incentives and Awards for Students

_____

_____

_____

Grand Total of Wish List   _____

Projected Award Amount _____

Difference   _____

Avoid a Budget Breakdown

- Use your dollars to fund goods and services that are not normally included in a school budget.
- Explain big-ticket items in great detail, relating the purchase to specific objectives.
- Attempt to bring in outside funds, say from the PTA or a local business, to supplement projected grant funds. This makes your project more fundable.
- Keep travel costs and training costs fairly low. These areas are a "red flag" to foundations. They don't like to pay for personnel to fly around the country unless it is unavoidable.
- Keep the budget focused on the students. Budget for items, services, and equipment that will directly change instruction and behaviors in your classes.
- Avoid a budget that looks like it is simply designed to buy big-ticket items, such as computers, playground equipment, or aquariums. Instead, focus on a change in curriculum and instruction, and take the focus off the big items.
- Always attach a contract for purchased services, such as speakers, bus trips, tickets to events.
- Include detailed job descriptions and projected time allowances for personnel.
- Some foundations will allow teachers to receive honoraria for services rendered. Others will allow the school to hire a substitute while the teacher works on the project.
- Read the guidelines for budget carefully, and do not deviate from them. Foundations and agencies know what kinds of things they want to fund. Don't try to sneak anything past them.
- Don't worry about small changes in budget after you are funded. You will have an opportunity to explain these things in your final budget report.
- Be scrupulous in the preparation of your final reports. A well-done final report puts you in good stead for future funding.

GA1515

Beat the Budget Blues

Answer each question carefully.

1. Did I relate major equipment purchases to specific objectives? Explain.

   _____

   _____

   _____

   Total Amount of Equipment _____
   Total in Budget _____

2. Is the budget robust enough to meet the goals of the project? Do we have enough personnel to make the thing work? Explain.

   _____

   _____

   _____

   Total Personnel Cost _____
   Total in Budget _____

3. Did I clearly explain how multiple items such as twenty microscopes or thirty calculators will be shared among several teachers? This kind of explanation makes it look like the money is going farther.

   _____

   _____

   _____

4. Is the budget focused on the goals of the program? For example, if your grant is for language arts, don't try to include calculators and science beakers unless you have clearly stated objectives that address the integration of other subject areas.

   _____

   _____

GA1515

Chapter Review

Test your budget expertise. Circle the answer that is most appropriate.

1. Which of these will weaken your budget the most?

   math errors   waste   items unrelated to objectives

2. Equipment is usually worth how much per item?

   $25 $100 $500

3. In-kind contributions are in the form of:

   whole dollars   pledges   goods and services

4. A consultant and a trip to the zoo have this in common:

   honoraria   not fundable   must attach contract

5. Items such as typewriters and office equipment are justifiable in your grant.

   always   sometimes   seldom

6. Which total is written correctly?

   $23,888.79 $23,000.99 $23,000

7. Supplies and other expendable items have an estimated usefulness of less than:

   6 months   2 years   1 year

Did you mark the last item in each list as the correct answer? If you missed more than two items, reread the glossary in Chapter 2 and all of Chapter 9.

GA1515

Chapter Ten

Editing Is Everything

Editing Is Everything

Completing a narrative that is solid, centered, and sharp gave you the focus for the first eight chapters of this text. Now, you should take a second, scrutinizing look at that same body of work. It is the time of reckoning. It is the time of culling, clipping, and clarifying. It is time to edit. And in grant writing, editing is everything.

Turn to the next page and look over the five Edicts for Editors, a simple set of ordinances that can make your proposal much more competitive and clear.

Edicts for Editors

1. Let the narrative rest for a minimum of two days before you attempt to proofread it or do any editing.

2. Use a reliable piece of "spell-checking" software and a "grammar checker" if both are available.

3. Have an unbiased colleague read the manuscript for clarity and content before you submit it.

4. Highlight the requirements for the narrative in your guidelines, and then match them against the finished manuscript as part of the editing process.

5. Make sure that the finished appearance of the manuscript is impeccable: dark, clear type; even margins; pages numbered; addenda identified.

****

Little Things That Make a Big Difference

1. Make copies of everything: letters of intent, addenda, test results, the budget. You would be amazed at how things can be misplaced and how many proposals miss the deadline because of a postal or administrative error. Always have a backup plan.

2. Don't be tempted to attach shoddy copies of addenda, thinking that it really doesn't matter. It does. Your attachments should be crisp and professional looking.

3. Always attach a Table of Contents to your proposal. It looks professional and organized.

4. When you are identifying a group of test scores or other data that takes more than two lines, box it in dark lines to set it apart.

GA1515

Catch the Most Common Errors

Remember edict number 3: having an unbiased colleague look at your work? Well, I applied that rule here, and asked my friend and fellow grant-writing instructor, Peggy Trivelas, to outline for me the most frequently seen errors in narratives. Peggy is a highly successful grant writer herself and has also assisted dozens of teachers in writing successful proposals. She teaches in Aiken, South Carolina, and is an adjunct professor at Charleston Southern University.

Ten Typical Errors in Grant Writing

1. Usage Errors:

   their or there or they're
   it's or its
   a or an

   Incorrect: Students will edit there own books.
   Correct: Students will edit their own books.

2. Subject-Verb Agreement

   Incorrect: A student who write stories will learn to be a better
              reader.
   Correct: A student who writes stories will learn to be a better
              reader.

3. Run-On Sentences

   Incorrect: Students solve problems they apply skills.
   Correct: Students solve problems. They apply skills.
              Students solve problems, and they apply skills.

4. Sentence Fragments

   Incorrect: For a classroom management system.
   Correct: This is a good idea for a classroom management system.

5. Pure Spelling Errors
   confution instead of *confusion*
   asessment instead of *assessment*
   mathmatics instead of *mathematics*
   arithematic instead of *arithmetic*

6. Incorrect Comma Usage with Independent Clauses
   Incorrect: Students will write their own stories and they will read them to the class.
   Correct: Students will write their own stories, and they will read them to the class.

7. Agreement Problems (number)

   Incorrect: Students write books and read it to the class.
              (books = plural   it = singular)
   Correct: Students write books and read them to the class.

8. Pronoun Agreement Problems

   Incorrect: Students find locations on a globe, then he writes the answer on a work sheet.
   Correct: Students find locations on a globe. Then one of the students writes the answer on the work sheet.

9. Apostrophe Errors
   Incorrect: One students book
              Several student's books
              Childrens' books
   Correct: One student's book
              Several students' books
              Children's books

10. Avoid "due to." It sounds like your bills are due. Instead, use "because of."

Weak: Students' math scores are low due to a lack of manipulatives in the classroom.

Better: Students' math scores are low because of a lack of manipulatives in the classroom.

****

Use a good quality guide for more detailed editing. I suggest one of the following:

1. *Publications Manual of the American Psychological Association.* Third Edition. Publishing information not available.

2. *The Harbrace College Handbook.* New York: Harcourt, Brace & Jovanovich, 1990.

3. *Edit Yourself: A Manual for Everyone Who Works with Words.* By Bruce Ross Larson. New York: W. W. Norton & Co., Inc., 1985.

Chapter Review

What could be a more appropriate review for the chapter on editing than to have you proof a sample of narrative that has been deliberately defiled? There are ten errors in this little piece of work. Circle the errors as you find them, and then rewrite the paragraph correctly.

****

The Sorry Sample

Third gradders at Southside Elementary School performs poorly on test of mathmatics and problem solving. They are weak in this area due to a lack of manipulatives in they're classrooms. On the new york Achievement Test, forty percent of the student could not solve basic word problems. A survey of teachers at the school showed that most teachers believes that greater access to manipulatives would help the students' to become more skilled in this area.

****

An Edited Example

_____

_____

_____

_____

_____

_____

_____

A Final Word on Editing: Don't overlook the importance of this section. Many teachers haven't written a lengthy document since graduate school. Skills become rusty, and writers become stressed and careless. Deadlines and demands intensify the incidence of errors. So, edit carefully. It might make the difference that takes you over the edge into funding.

GA1515

Chapter Eleven

$$$$$ Funding Sources $$$$$

Writing a persuasive narrative and plotting a good budget are only part of the battle of grant writing. Your strategy should be based on the prospective *source* of funding. In other words, you tailor your grant to fit the funding plans of the agency or foundation.

Here are a few techniques for linking up with funding sources.

****

1. Initiate a *relationship* with the foundation or project director. Talk on the telephone and correspond by mail. Get to know this person, because he or she represents the grantor and can best advise you on preparing your proposal.
2. After initiating the contact by phone (preferably) and/or by mail, send a *letter of intent* and an *abstract* of the proposal to see if there is interest.
3. Ask for a set of guidelines and find out if there are any *program limitations*. This simply means a limit on the kinds of programs that can be funded or the region in which programs can be funded.

****

In your grant-writing library or the professional shelf in your school library, there are a few books that are important and helpful to teachers who want to seek grants.

1. *Annual Register of Grant Support: A Directory of Funding Sources.* Published by Macmillian Directory Division, 3004 Glenview Rd., Wilmette, IL 60091. Nicely indexed by title and type of projects funded.

2. *Catalog of Federal Domestic Assistance*. Call 202-783-3238 and subscribe to this 1000-page document that gives you a complete outline of government-sponsored grants that you can apply for.

3. *The Foundation Directory*. Call 800-424-9836. This is a reliable asset of information on over 6000 funders.

4. *The Federal Register*. U.S. Government Printing Office, Washington, DC 20402.

5. *The Catalogue of the National Diffusion Network*. Call 303-651-2829. This unique book offers a listing and description of hundreds of "exemplary" programs that have already been successful around the country. Sometimes, a validated program has a better chance of funding than one that you are testing out on your own.

6. *The National Guide to Funding for Elementary and Secondary Education*. Call 800-424-9836. This is a unique source with over 4000 listings.

7. *Education Grants Alert*. (newsletter) Call 800-327-7203. Easy to use, especially for beginners.

Funding Sources for Teachers

1. Apple Community Affairs
   20525 Mariana Ave.
   Cupertino, CA 95014

   • Funds computer equipment and software for schools

2. Exxon Education Foundation
   225 East John W. Carpenter Freeway
   Irving, TX 75062-2298

   • Innovative math programs and K-12 math curriculum

3. Mattel Foundation
   333 Continental Blvd.
   El Segundo, CA 90245

   • Special Ed. K-12 Young Children Learning Labs

4. National Endowment for the Humanities
   1100 Pennsylvania Ave. NW
   Washington, DC 20506

   • Ask for school grants for cultural/arts programs.

5. National Science Foundation
   1800 G. St. NW
   Washington, DC 20550

   • Ask for school grants for innovative science programs.

6. Quaker Oats Foundation
   P.O. Box 9001
   Chicago, IL 60604-9001

   • Youth programs, school reform, arts/cultural projects for children

7. Tandy Corp./Radio Shack
   1600 One Tandy Center
   Fort Worth, TX 76102

   • Equipment and software gifts to schools

8. Texaco Foundation
   2000 Westchester Ave.
   White Plains, NY 10650

   • Innovations in schools and programs for deprived kids

GA1515

9. Toshiba America Foundation
   375 Park Avenue
   New York, NY 10152

   • Improvements in science and science related curricula

10. Wells Fargo Bank
    101 California Street
    San Francisco, CA 94163

    • Restructuring efforts in K-12 schools

11. Westinghouse Foundation
    West Building Gateway Center
    Pittsburgh, PA 15222

    • Ask for guidelines for teacher/school grants in the areas of science, child welfare, and cultural ed.

12. Wettereau Inc.
    8920 Pershall Road
    Hazelwood, MO 63042-2809

    • Inquire with proposals for family projects, children in crises, or school improvements.

****

• Ask for specific program guidelines.

• Try to work with companies that have some local branch or affiliation.

• Hook up with a local college or university to submit a proposal together.

• Send a letter of intent and abstract before you sink a lot of time into a full proposal.

• Choose one teacher or administrator to conduct the calls and inquiries so that you do not appear to be disorganized.

Note: Every effort has been made, at the time of publication, to insure the accuracy of the information included in this book. We cannot guarantee, however, that the agencies and organizations we have mentioned will continue to operate or to maintain these current locations indefinitely.

GA1515

Sample Letter of Intent

Anytown Middle School
Sunnyvale, South Carolina 29432
Office of the Principal

United States Department of Energy
Washington, DC
Project PREP Coordinator

Dear Dr. Smythe:

It is our intent to submit a proposal for an innovative mathematics and science program for middle school-aged girls from a rural school district in South Carolina. Anytown Middle School serves 723 students in grades 5-8.

I would like to request project guidelines for such a program. The enclosed abstract gives you a brief overview of the planned initiative and information about the collaborating partners.

Please forward all future correspondence to me, Laura Jones. I will be serving as the coordinator of the project. In addition, I would be happy to talk with you by telephone. You can reach me at school, after 3:00 p.m., at (803) 821-1130. Thank you.

Yours truly,

Laura Jones

Laura Jones

Sample Abstract

Department of Energy: Project PREP
Project Duration 1994-1996

The School of Education and the Department of Natural Sciences at Anytown University, in collaboration with Anytown Middle School, seek funds to continue the Pre-Freshman Enrichment Program efforts that have been successfully implemented for two years.

Careful evaluation of the first cycle of funding reveals that positive gains were made by the thirty youngsters who were involved in the project. Moreover, the gains appear to be significant in both academic and social development. Based on this data, which is detailed in the narrative of the proposal, the collaborative has reorganized and enhanced the objectives for a new cycle of PREP.

The revised program is based on four innovations. First, the target population will be young women from a rural, economically disadvantaged school district, who demonstrate interest and academic potential for science-based careers. Second, the young women will work in cooperative learning groups during the two-year duration of the project. Third, the cooperative learning groups will apply knowledge in mathematics and science to design a Field Analysis Test Kit during year one of the project, and will then use the Field Analysis Test Kit in a series of controlled laboratory and field experiences during the second year of the project. Fourth, the evaluation of the students' work will be measured using a portfolio technique, rather than test data.

In addition, Project PREP at Anytown University contains a strong teacher-training component. Three teachers from the participating district will work with university faculty in the five-week day program. These teachers can then return to the district with new methods and materials to enhance their teaching. Also, a group of thirty undergraduate intern teachers will use the PREP site to complete practicum experiences during the summer. These interns will offer the PREP students individual attention and a wide variety of enrichment opportunities.

Finally, PREP draws on the talents of local business and industry to round out the summer project with a weekly motivational component. Successful young female engineers and researchers will visit the PREP site to give motivational talks to the students. Field trips to business and industry will complete the motivational component.

Cooperative learning teams, portfolio evaluation, the business and industry connection, and an academic component that is firmly based in research and problem-solving make this PREP project active, participatory, and valuable to the young women who might never have the opportunity to see themselves as engineers, doctors, scientists, or mathematicians in the year 2000.

GA1515

A Sample Grant

GA1515

Take a Look at a Sample Grant

Grant Writing for Teachers has been designed to take you step-by-step through the process of creating a strong narrative and a solid budget. Although the process is organized, details and ideas can become jumbled as one writes and rewrites. Looking at a sample grant, one that was written by an actual teacher who used the techniques outlined in this text, may clear up some of your questions. Vicki Taylor, who teaches compensatory reading at Spann Elementary School in Summerville, South Carolina, wrote this proposal during a graduate course on grant writing. Peggy Trivelas and I taught the course. Special thanks to Dorchester School District Two, Joe Pye, Charlie Stoudenmire, Carolyn Daniels and especially Vicki Taylor, for their contributions to this sample grant.

****

Take Note of the Following as You Read

1. How the title of the grant is used frequently
2. How the title is catchy and fun–"Spanda Satchels" is a take-off on the name of the school (Spann) and the school mascot (a panda)
3. Timely quotes from a respected journal in the problem area (justification)
4. A strong letter of support from an expert
5. Matching objectives and evaluation
6. A checklist that is appropriately attached
7. Thorough and detailed activities
8. Clearly itemized budget

GA1515

SECTION III–Project Summary

At Spann Elementary School, compensatory reading students will take "Spanda Satchels" home to share with their families. Each satchel will contain a variety of reading materials and related activities. Fifty-three students are assigned to the compensatory program based on poor test performance. They generally have negative attitudes toward reading. This project will improve reading skills and fluency, as well as students' attitudes. As a result, reading scores on the BSAP test will increase. During my experience as a second and third grade compensatory reading teacher, my observations supported the research concerning the connection between independent reading and reading achievement. "Spanda Satchels" will put high interest reading material in the hands of children who need tangible, immediate reinforcement for their efforts. The project will build self-worth as well as academics.

GA1515

SECTION IV–Problem Area

Reading is a complex process. Abundant practice is necessary before competency is achieved. Evidence indicates that special needs children read only a limited amount. This problem is addressed in my innovative proposal, "Spanda Satchels."

Research reveals a strong connection between independent reading and reading achievement. In the November/December 1991 issue of *The Clearing House*, Farris and Hancock write, "Time spent reading books is closely associated with the measure of a child's status as a reader. Reading books has been found to be a cause, not merely a reflection, of reading proficiency." (Addendum I) Yet many children read very little. As Richek and McTague state in the December 1988 issue of *The Reading Teacher*, "Poor readers are not reading enough to learn to read well." (Addendum II) In the March 1991 issue of *The Reading Teacher*, Richek and Glick write, "This practice is particularly lamentable for children in many remedial programs who read less and do more worksheets than normally achieving peers." (Addendum III) Farris and Hancock write, "For the majority of subjects, reading books occupied only one percent or less of their leisure time." (Addendum I)

Spann compensatory students completed the Elementary Reading Attitude Survey (Addendum IV) in February 1993. The average score was 53, which ranks at the 32nd percentile. Moreover, there was a six point difference between recreational reading and academic reading scores. This difference suggests that students ". . . may not have been exposed to a variety of interesting trade books." (Addendum IV)

BSAP READING SCORES: SECOND GRADE

1989-90	1990-91	1991-92
94	93	92

A review of three years of data reveals a continual decline in BSAP reading scores. (Addendum V)

Finally, my proposal has attracted the attention of Carolyn Daniel, President of the Dorchester Reading Council, whose letter of support is attached. (Addendum VI)

SDE 25-028-00

(This form becomes obsolete 6/30/95.)

GA1515

SECTION V—Statement of Goals and Objectives

Goal:

The goal of "Spanda Satchels" is to improve compensatory students' reading skills, fluency, and attitudes at Spann Elementary School.

Objectives:

1. On the BSAP reading test, compensatory students will demonstrate improved reading skills and fluency.
2. Students will read books and complete the activities in a minimum of thirty "Spanda Satchels."
3. Students' scores on the Elementary Reading Attitude Survey will increase.

SECTION VI—Evaluation Plan

1. On the BSAP reading test, 80 percent of the compensatory reading students will demonstrate improved reading skills and fluency by scoring above 700.

2. Students will read books and complete activities in a minimum of thirty "Spanda Satchels." Progress will be recorded on the Spanda Satchel Activity Checklist. (Addendum VII)

3. On the Elementary Reading Attitude Survey (Addendum IV), 90 percent of the students will score above the sixtieth percentile.

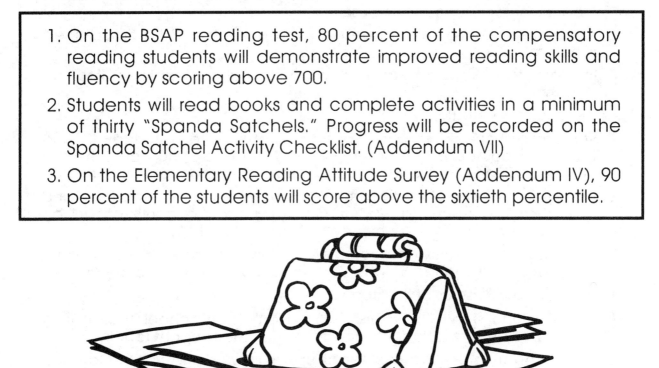

SDE 25-028-00
(This form becomes obsolete 6/30/95.)

SECTION VII—Description of Activities

I. Preparation:

   A. Bookbags—canvas totebags (14" x 10$^1/_2$") with "Spanda Satchel" silkscreened logo. Bags will include:

      1. High-interest hardcover Perma-Bound books appropriate for second and third grade students.

      2. A pocket folder that contains activities that reinforce and enrich the skills and themes related to the book. Activities will emphasize higher order thinking skills, phonics, creative writing, and reading skills.

      3. A packet of information from the Dorchester and Charleston County Libraries describing services available to local residents and applications for library cards.

      4. A copy of *The Read Aloud Handbook* by Jim Trelease will circulate among the "Spanda Satchels." This will allow families access to a list of recommended reading material for children.

II. Explanation of Program:

   A. A teacher in-service will be conducted to explain the "Spanda Satchel" program.

   B. A "Spanda Satchel" will be placed in the Spann Elementary School Media Center for teachers to use.

   C. A meeting with parents will be held to discuss the "Spanda Satchel" program.

   D. In class, the "Spanda Satchel" program will be explained to the students.

III. Program Implementation:

   A. Students will check out one "Spanda Satchel" every Monday. During the week, parents and children will read the book and complete the corresponding activities. The "Spanda Satchel" will be returned Friday.

   B. Upon return of the "Spanda Satchel," students will receive a sticker and have their "Frequent Reader Club Card" punched. A certificate will be awarded for every five satchels completed successfully.

   C. The teacher will review the completed activities and evaluate student progress on the Spanda Satchel Activity Checklist. (Addendum VII)

IV. Additional Components of Program:

   A. A professional storyteller will visit Spann Elementary School twice during the year to entertain students and promote independent reading.

   B. The compensatory reading teacher will attend the South Carolina International Reading Association Conference in February 1995.

SDE 25-028-00
(This form becomes obsolete 6/30/95.)

GA1515

SECTION VIII–Time Line

August:	Order materials.
September:	1. Assemble "Spanda Satchels."
	2. Conduct teacher in-service to discuss "Spanda Satchel" program.
	3. Place a "Spanda Satchel" in the media center for teachers' use.
	4. Meet with parents to discuss the "Spanda Satchel" program.
	5. Explain "Spanda Satchels" to the students.
October:	Implement the "Spanda Satchel" program.
November:	A professional storyteller will visit and entertain the students.
February:	Attend the South Carolina I.R.A. Conference.
March:	A professional storyteller will visit and entertain the students.
May:	Prepare final report of "Spanda Satchel" program.

SECTION IX–Exportable Product Description

The exportable product will be a "Spanda Satchel" which will be placed in the Spann Elementary School Media Center. The "Spanda Satchel" may be used by interested teachers. The satchel will contain a copy of *The Read Aloud Handbook* by Jim Trelease; a list of recommended reading material for second and third grade students; a list of resource materials; and a packet detailing the "Spanda Satchel" program, its components, circulation, and management.

SDE 25-028-00
(This form becomes obsolete 6/30/95.)

Budget for the "Spanda Satchel" Program

Salaries

Substitute Teacher, 1 day $ 40.00

Benefits

Benefits for Substitute Teacher $ 7.00

Purchased Services

Margie Clary, Storyteller	$ 200.00
Silkscreening for Bags	84.00
I.R.A. Conference (registration and room)	115.00
Total	$ 399.00

Supplies and Materials

The Highsmith Co., Inc.
W5527 Highway 106
P.O. Box 800
Fort Atkinson, WI 53538-0800

60 Canvas Totebags L51-56190 Color R	$ 212.00
Shipping	12.00
Total	$ 224.00

Wal-Mart
Rivers Avenue
Charleston, SC 29420

5 Packages Shower Curtain Hooks (12/pkg.) $ 7.00

GA1515

Supplies and Materials

Stone's School Supply, Inc.
P.O. Box 37307
Raleigh, NC 27627-7307

1 Big Book of Stickers IF4120	$ 20.00
4 Pkg. Frequent Readers Club Cards TSD 2070-5	16.00
5 Pkg. Reading Award Certificates T-392	10.00
4 Pkg. Special Reader Certificates T-393	8.00
3 Boxes Two-Pocket Folders (25/box)	33.00
1 *The Caldecott Award* Book TSD 1718-6	11.00
1 *Newbery and Caldecott Books in the Classroom* Book IP 194-0	13.00
3 *Literature and Critical Thinking* Books TCM 311, TCM 317, TCM 357	30.00
Subtotal	$ 141.00
Shipping	$ 5.00
Total	$ 146.00

Perma-Bound Books
Vandalia Road
Jacksonville, IL 62650

2 New *Read Aloud Handbook* by Jim Trelease	$ 28.00
1 Caldecott Medal and Honor Books 1992	38.00
1 Caldecott Medal and Honor Books 1991	51.00
1 Caldecott Medal and Honor Books 1990	86.00
1 Caldecott Medal and Honor Books 1988	36.00
1 Caldecott Medal Winners	501.00
Subtotal	$ 740.00
Shipping	$ 37.00
Total	$ 777.00

Equipment

The Highsmith Co., Inc.
W5527 Highway 106
P.O. Box 800
Fort Atkinson, WI 53538-0800

1 Three-Tier Hanging Bag Tree L51-10603	$ 390.00
Shipping	10.00
Total	$ 400.00
TOTAL EXPENDITURES	$2000.00

GA1515

DORCHESTER READING COUNCIL
SUMMERVILLE, SOUTH CAROLINA

March 3, 1993

Carolyn M. Daniel
President, Dorchester Reading Council
Chapter I Reading
Givhans Elementary School
Rt 3, Hway 61
Ridgeville SC 29472

To whom it may concern:

As president of the Dorchester Reading Council in Summerville, South Carolina, I am writing you on behalf of Ms. Vicki Taylor. Not only is she a fine teacher, but she has written an EIA grant for a proposal that I believe worthy of full funding.

Ms. Taylor proposes a project that is designed to target the 53 compensatory reading students at Spann Elementary School, here in Summerville. She has become aware of a problem that I have faced frequently: too often, these "at-risk" students have parents who are themselves under-educated adults. These are the children who rarely have any high-interest reading materials in their homes, and they are the children who seldom experience the pleasure of having a story read to them. With your help and funding, Ms. Taylor's project can help alleviate that problem.

In its 1985 report, the Commission on Education reported that the single most important activity for building the knowledge required for eventual success in reading is to read aloud to children. The commission also found conclusive evidence to support the concept that reading aloud at home is just as vital as reading at school. Various other research studies have provided evidence of the direct relationship between reading aloud to children and reading performance, language development, and the development of reading interest. By reading aloud to children, parents can provoke a curiosity about books and they can let their children know that they place a high value on literacy.

Ms. Taylor's proposed project, "Spanda Satchels," can play a vital role in our efforts to reach all of our students. I believe programs like this one provide us with the tools we need to eliminate the inter-generational illiteracy that pervades far too many of the families in our community.

Please, give this proposal your most careful consideration for full funding. Thank you.

Sincerely,

Carolyn M. Daniel

GA1515

Spanda Satchel Activity Checklist

Name _____

Name of Satchel	Date Completed	S	N	U	NC

Key:

S   Satisfactory

N   Needs Improvement

U   Unsatisfactory

NC   Not Completed

GA1515

Chapter Review

I hope you enjoyed Vicki Taylor's proposal. She applied the techniques appropriately and came out with a strong grant. However, as we end this book, I'd like to take a few lines to point out the "hidden agenda" of grant writing. It is a troubling, yet real, aspect of the game that must be addressed.

The Hidden Agenda

1. Even a well-written, well-designed proposal may not be funded. There are limited dollars in each "pot" and your funding may often hinge on sheer numbers. That is, how many other proposals were considered?
2. Sometimes politics and priorities take precedence. If a particular foundation or agency decides to give priority to, say, "science grants" this year, and you have an excellent "language arts grant," then you may not be funded.
3. Demographics can be influential. If you are applying for a grant from a foundation that has already funded a significant proposal in your area of the country, then perhaps you should reconsider the proposal. Folks like to spread the money out, unless you are applying to a foundation that specifically funds only in your region. Check the *Foundation Directory*.
4. Try, try again. Foundations and agencies may want to "get to know you" with the first round of proposals. Don't get discouraged. Ask for feedback and take it seriously. Then, apply again.
5. Keep a positive attitude. Nothing is ever a waste in grant writing. The research, writing, and planning will help you to become a more effective educator, whether or not you are funded the first time out. Grant writing is part of growing as a professional. As we all know, growing is a sometimes painful as well as pleasurable process. Good luck to all of you.